The Wicca Spellbook

Also by Gerina Dunwich

The Wicca Spellbook

by Gerina Dunwich

CITADEL PRESS
Kensington Publishing Corp.
www.kensingtonbooks.com

CITADEL PRESS books are published by

Kensington Publishing Corp.
850 Third Avenue
New York, NY 10022

All Kensington titles, imprints, and distributed lines are available at special quantity discounts for bulk purchases for sales promotions, premiums, fund-raising, educational, or institutional use. Special book excerpts or customized printings can also be created to fit specific needs. For details, write or phone the office of the Kensington special sales manager: Kensington Publishing Corp., 850 Third Avenue, New York, NY 10022, attn: Special Sales Department, phone 1-800-221-2647.

Citadel Press and the Citadel logo are trademarks of Kensington Publishing Corp.

First Kensington printing August 2001

10   9   8   7   6   5   4   3   2   1

Printed in the United States of America

Cataloging data for this title may be obtained from the Library of Congress.

ISBN 0-8065-1470-0

This book is dedicated with love to my Mother; Al B. Jackter; Barbara Jacobson; Lisa Faulkner; Farika; and the immortal spirit of Wilva. May the Gods of Old bless you with an abundance of Magick, Mirth, and Love.

I also wish to express my deepest gratitude to the Goddess for Her divine inspiration and guidance, and to all at Carol Publishing Group for making this book possible.

Blessed Be!

The Magick Circle

Circle of starlight,
Circle of fire,
filled with enchantments
bright with desire.
  Turning, turning,
  beginning to end;
  end to beginning
  again and again.

Circle of wisdom,
Circle of love,
silver with moonbeams
  bright from above.
Circle of death,
Circle of re-birth,
Circle of the Mother Earth.

Shining, shining,
forever and ever.
Spinning, spinning,
ending never.
Weaving the threads
of the midnight hour.
Weaving the web of Goddess power.

—from *Words of the Cosmic Winds*
by Gerina Dunwich

Contents

Introduction

What Is Wicca?

Wicca is a positive journey to enlightenment through Goddess-worship and the mystical art of white magick. It is a shamanistic nature-oriented religion and a unique and exciting blend of the traditional and the eclectic that seeks neither to convert, conform, or control.

Unlike many other religions, Wicca does not claim to be the one and only way for everybody, and it does not campaign against other religious traditions (although the other way around is unfortunately the case at times).

Wicca is not anti-Christian; however, it does not acknowledge the existence of sin, the Devil, or a judgmental and avenging god as defined by Christianity.

Wicca encourages free thought, artistic creativity, individuality, and personal, spiritual, and psychic growth. It is a celebration of the cycle of seasons and of life. Wicca is respecting and living in harmony with all living things. Wicca is Light. Wicca is Love. Wicca is called the "Craft of the Wise" and is both ancient and new. It is a path unlike any other in the world.

What Is Magick?

Magick is difficult to define. The dictionary calls it "the art of persons who claim to be able to do things by the help of supernatural powers or by their own knowledge of nature's secrets." Most Wiccans and Neo-Pagans alike would agree that although magick might appear to be "supernatural," it is a power or force that is quite natural.

For many people a first impression of magick is that it is all "bell, book and candle," but upon closer examination, they find that there is more to it than magickal paraphernalia. (The tools of the Craft are merely "props" serving as sources to help focus power.) Magick is a wondrous energy that is raised through various means (meditation, dancing, and ritual sex, to name a few) and then psychically directed at a specific goal—to heal an illness, attract love, or remedy a bad situation.

Magick is "the use of will to effect some desired change"; therefore, any open-minded human being who possesses the ability to focus and concentrate their will is capable of working successful magick. Some folks need to practice often to get their magickal skills fine-tuned, while others are blessed with more of a natural aptitude for it.

Magick is a state of mind and a Goddess-given gift that plays a major role in the religion of Wicca. It is the Witch's contact with the Divine. It is the Witch's prayer.

Just as there are many different ways to define magick, there are also many different ways to perceive it. Magick is all around us, and within us. It radiates in all things that live and die. It can be felt in a baby's first breath and in the changing of the seasons. It is a part of the Earth, the mysterious ocean, and the starlit heavens above us. There is magick in love and magick in dreams. It can be found on a hill of wildflowers dancing in the sun-drenched breeze, in the cool shadows of some quiet enchanted woodland, or in the lines of a beautiful poem. All you need to do is open your heart.

> "AN IT HARM NONE, LOVE,
> AND DO WHAT THOU WILT!"
> —*THE WICCAN REDE*

1

Gerina's Grimoire

"An it harm none, do what thou wilt."

These eight simple words make up the Wiccan Rede, which is the main tenet of the Wiccan religion. What it means, quite simply, is: be free to practice the arts of magick, develop and utilize your psychic powers, and do your own thing, provided that no harm comes to anyone as a result.

It is imperative to bear in mind the Wiccan Rede before performing any magickal spells or rituals, especially those which may be considered unethical or of a manipulative nature.

If you violate the Wiccan Rede (even unintentionally), bad karma will instantly come back to you, whether you believe in it or not.

There is much truth in the expression, "What goes around, comes around," so you should be very careful and think twice before using magick or psychic powers to "get even" with an enemy. Always deal with problems by using positive magickal energy rather than concentrating on the negative.

If you deliberately harm or manipulate another person through black magick or any form of evil, you will pay for it by having the evil return to you threefold.

By the same token, whenever you do something positive or good (such as a healing or helping spell), it will result in threefold good karma instantly returned to you.

This Karmic law of retribution is known as the Threefold Law (or the Law of Three) and I've seen it work many times with my very own eyes—even to persons who once thought that instant karma was just the title of a song.

If you feel it *is* necessary, please feel free to make minor changes or additions to any spell in this chapter to suit your individual needs. (Herbs, oils, incense, and so forth may be substituted with other material as long as the magickal properties remain the same. Do not, however, change the lunar phase in which a spell is intended to be performed, or the results of that spell will be altered.)

After performing a spell or magick ritual, I always give thanks to the Goddess and Her consort for their divine presence and protection. This is usually followed by a relaxing meditation ritual.

Lunar Magick

To most Wiccans and Neo-Pagans, the Moon is more than just a crater-covered natural satellite that revolves around the Earth and lights up the night sky.

The Moon is a bearer of omens, and a sacred symbol of Nature's cycle of life to death to rebirth. It represents the feminine principle, personified by the Triple Goddess (Maiden, Mother, and Crone of wisdom).

The connection between the mystical energy of the Moon and the Craft of the Wise dates back to early times when Witches were believed by many to possess a supernatural ability to literally "draw down the Moon" from the heavens and use it as the source of their magickal power.

The Moon and each of its phases are the most essential parts of modern Wiccan magick, so it is extremely important that all of your spells and rituals are performed during the proper lunar phase. (Performing a magickal spell during the wrong lunar phase could give you the opposite result or no result at all. Therefore, it only makes sense to check with an up-to-date astrological or lunar calendar before casting a spell of any kind.)

All spells and rituals that attract should be performed when the Moon is on the increase. All spells and rituals that banish should be performed when the Moon is on the decrease.

All spells and rituals that involve the element of fire should be performed when the Moon is positioned in one of the three astrological fire signs: Aries, Leo, Sagittarius.

All spells and rituals that involve the element of earth (such as Gaia-healing) should be performed when the Moon is positioned in one of the three astrological earth signs: Taurus, Virgo, Capricorn.

All spells and rituals that involve the element of air should be performed when the Moon is positioned in one of the three astrological air signs: Gemini, Libra, Aquarius.

All spells and rituals that involve the element of water should be performed when the Moon is positioned in one of the three astrological water signs: Cancer, Scorpio, Pisces.

WAXING MOON: The time from the New Moon through the first quarter to the Full Moon is the proper time to perform healing rituals, positive magick, and spells that increase love, good luck, growth of any kind, sexual desire, and wealth.

FULL MOON: The period of the Full Moon increases the powers of extrasensory perception, and is the proper time to perform lunar goddess invocations, fertility rituals, transformations, spirit conjurations, and spells that increase psychic abilities and prophetic dreams. According to ancient European folklore, the power of the Full Moon can also magickally transform man into beast, and beast into man.

WANING MOON: The time from the Full Moon through the last quarter to the New Moon is the proper time to perform destructive magick and spells that remove curses, hexes, and jinxes, end bad relationships, reverse love spells and aphrodisiacs, break bad habits and unhealthy addictions, undo negative influences, and decrease fevers and pains.

MOON IN ARIES   is the ideal time to cast spells that involve authority, leadership, willpower, warfare, and spiritual conversion or rebirth. It is also the proper lunar phase in which to perform healing rituals for ailments of the face, head, or brain. *Traditional candle colors:* red, crimson, scarlet, burgundy. *Traditional metal:* iron. *Elemental spirits:* salamanders.

MOON IN TAURUS is the ideal time to practice all forms of love magick, and to cast spells that involve real estate, material acquisitions, and money. It is also the proper lunar phase in which to perform healing rituals for ailments of the throat, neck, or ears. *Traditional candle colors*: all shades of green, pink, turquoise. *Traditional metal*: copper. *Elemental spirits*: gnomes.

MOON IN GEMINI is the ideal time to cast spells that involve communication, change of residence, writing, public relations activities, and travel. It is also the proper lunar phase in which to perform healing rituals for ailments of the shoulders, arms, hands, or lungs. *Traditional candle color*: mauve. *Traditional metal*: mercury. *Elemental spirits*: sylphs.

MOON IN CANCER is the ideal time to perform rituals honoring lunar deities, and to cast spells that involve the home and all aspects of domestic life. It is also the proper lunar phase in which to perform healing rituals for ailments of the chest or stomach. *Traditional candle colors*: silver, gray, white. *Traditional metal*: silver. *Elemental spirits*: undines.

MOON IN LEO is the ideal time to cast spells that involve authority, power over others, courage, fertility, and childbirth. It is also the proper lunar phase in which to perform healing rituals for ailments of the upper back, spine, or heart. *Traditional candle colors*: gold, yellow, orange. *Traditional metal*: gold. *Elemental spirits*: salamanders.

MOON IN VIRGO is the ideal time to cast spells that involve employment, intellectual matters, health, and dietary concerns. It is also the proper lunar phase in which to perform healing rituals for ailments of the intestines or nervous system. *Traditional candle colors*: navy blue, rust-orange. *Traditional metal:* mercury. *Elemental spirits:* gnomes.

MOON IN LIBRA   is the ideal time to cast spells that involve artistic work, justice, court cases, partnerships and unions, mental stimulation, and karmic, spiritual, or emotional balance. It is also the proper lunar phase in which to perform healing rituals for ailments of the lower back or kidneys. *Traditional candle color:* royal blue. *Traditional metal:* copper. *Elemental spirits:* sylphs.

MOON IN SCORPIO   is the ideal time to cast spells that involve sexual matters, power, psychic growth, secrets, and fundamental transformations. It is also the proper lunar phase in which to perform healing rituals for ailments of the reproductive organs. *Traditional candle colors:* red, black. *Traditional metal:* iron. *Elemental spirits:* undines.

MOON IN SAGITTARIUS   is the ideal time to cast spells that involve horses, travel, publications, legal matters, sports activities, and truth. It is also the proper lunar phase in which to perform healing rituals for ailments of the liver, thighs, or hips. *Traditional candle colors:* purple, dark blue. *Traditional metal:* tin. *Elemental spirits:* salamanders.

MOON IN CAPRICORN   is the ideal time to cast spells that involve organization, ambition, recognition, career, and political matters. It is also the proper lunar phase in which to perform healing rituals for ailments of the knees, bones, teeth, or skin. *Traditional candle colors:* black, dark brown. *Traditional metal:* lead. *Elemental spirits:* gnomes.

MOON IN AQUARIUS is the ideal time to cast spells that involve science, freedom, creative expression, problem-solving, extrasensory abilities, friendship, and the breaking of bad habits or unhealthy addictions. It is also the proper lunar phase in which to perform healing rituals for ailments of the calves, ankles, or blood. *Traditional candle color:* light blue. *Traditional metal:* uranium. *Elemental spirits:* sylphs.

MOON IN PISCES is the ideal time to cast spells that involve dreamwork, clairvoyance, telepathy, music, and the creative arts. It is also the proper lunar phase in which to perform healing rituals for ailments of the feet or lymph glands. *Traditional candle colors:* aquamarine, lavender. *Traditional metal:* tin. *Elemental spirits:* undines.

Basic Candle Spell

Take a candle of the appropriate color (see the list of candle colors and their corresponding magickal properties below) and anoint it by rubbing a drop or two of myrrh oil on it. Using a straight pin, scratch your desire into the wax and then light the candle and allow it to burn itself completely out.

That's all there is to it. This is a very simple, yet highly potent spell.

BLACK: Meditation rituals, hexwork, uncrossing rituals and spells to banish evil entities and negative forces.

BLUE: Magick that involves honor, loyalty, peace, tranquillity, truth, wisdom, protection during sleep, astral projection, and spells to induce prophetic dreams.

BROWN: Spells to locate lost objects, improve powers of concentration and telepathy, and for protection of familiars and household pets.

GOLD: Spells that attract the power of cosmic influences, and rituals to honor solar deities.

GRAY: Spells to neutralize negative influences.

GREEN: Spells involving fertility, success, good luck, prosperity, money, rejuvenation, and ambition, and rituals to counteract greed and jealousy.

ORANGE: Spells to stimulate energy.

PINK: Love spells and rituals involving friendship or femininity.

PURPLE: Psychic manifestations, healing, and spells involving power, success, independence, and household protection.

RED: Fertility rites, aphrodisiacs, and spells involving sexual passion, love, health, physical strength, revenge, anger, willpower, courage, and magnetism.

SILVER: Spells and rituals to remove negativity, encourage stability, and attract the influence of the Goddess.

WHITE: Consecration rituals, meditation, divination, exorcism, and spells that involve healing, clairvoyance, truth, peace, spiritual strength, and lunar energy.

YELLOW: Spells involving confidence, attraction, charm, and persuasion.

Love Magick

PHOTOGRAPH SPELL: When the Moon is waxing and love is in the air, take a photograph of the man or woman from whom you desire affections and place it face up in a small pink box (an empty heart-shaped candy box is perfect), then cover it with the herb known as ladies thumb. Cover the box and bury it outside next to the front entrance of your home to draw your beloved to you.

TO MAKE LOVE SECURE: Take a lock of hair and/or some fingernail clippings from your lover or spouse, and by the light of a pink, strawberry-scented candle, place them in a hollowed-out apple along with a dried and ground unicorn root, pansy flowers or spikenard, and a lock of your own hair. Pass the apple through the smoke of frankincense and myrrh; wrap it in a piece of white satin; and then bury it in your backyard. (If you do not have a backyard, you can bury the apple in a large flowerpot, preferably one in which a Venus-ruled plant is growing. For a complete list of plants ruled by Venus, please see my book, *The Secrets of Love Magick*.)

TO ATTRACT THE OPPOSITE SEX: Brew a magickal tea from gentian, marigold, passionflower, rue, sumbul root, or violets. Strain and add some to your bathwater for seven nights in a row.

To Keep Your Lover Faithful

There are many simple, yet highly effective, magickal methods that a Witch can use to ensure that her lover or spouse remains true to her. Five of those methods are as follows:

1. Brew tea from senna herb; strain and pour the liquid into the water of your lover's bath without his or her knowledge.

2. Sprinkle some powdered licorice herb over the footprints of your lover or spouse.

3. Moisten a small amount of linden herb on the palm of your right hand and then dab it on your lover's forehead when he or she is sleeping.

4. Place a handful of marigolds or rosemary in, around, and underneath the bed in which your lover or spouse sleeps.

5. Mix some cumin into your lover's food or drink to keep him or her faithful, especially if you are to be separated for long periods of time.

Aphrodite Love Spell

To attract the love of a particular gentleman or lady, perform this love spell on a Friday evening, preferably when the Moon is in the astrological sign of Taurus:

On a pink, heart-shaped piece of paper, write the full name of your beloved in red ink. To make the spell even more potent, write his or her birthdate or astrological symbol under the name.

Light a stick or cone of jasmine, lemon, myrrh, orange blossom, patchouli, or strawberry incense. Place it in a fireproof burner, and say:

> APHRODITE, APHRODITE,
> GODDESS OF LOVE
> AND PASSION MIGHTY,
> LOOK DOWN FROM ABOVE
> AND HEAR MY PRAYER.
> GRANT ME A LOVE
> SO TRUE AND SO FAIR.

With a sterilized pin or needle, prick the tip of your left thumb, squeeze out a drop of blood, and smear it over the name on the paper.

Place a pink votive candle (or a small male or female-shaped candle, depending upon the gender of your intended lover) over the paper. Light the candle and say thrice:

> WITH BLOOD AND FIRE
> THE MAGICK BEGINS.
> NOW PANGS OF DESIRE
> BURN FROM WITHIN.

Focus all of your thoughts and psychic energy upon your beloved, and say:

BEAT FOR ME NOW, O MORTAL HEART,
ACHE FOR ME NOW WHEN WE'RE APART,
DREAM OF ME IN THE MOONLIT NIGHT,
COME TO ME WHEN THE SUN SHINES BRIGHT.
SO MOTE IT BE!

Continue concentrating on the object of your affections until the incense and the candle burn themselves out.

Dream Spells for Lovers

To induce prophetic dreams about your future lover or marriage mate, perform any of the following dream spells:

1. On a night when the Moon is full and bright, take "The Lovers" card from a Tarot deck and place it underneath your pillow before going to sleep.

2. Collect nine leaves from a female holly at the stroke of midnight on a Friday (the day of the week ruled by Venus, the goddess of love). Place them in a three-cornered handkerchief tied with three knots, and place the charm under your pillow before you retire. (Be careful not to utter even one word until the following sunrise or else the power of the charm will be broken.)

3. An old dream-spell from Ireland calls for the gathering of ten ivy leaves in silence on a Samhain eve. Cast one leaf into a fire and place the remaining ones under your pillow before you go to bed.

4. Place any of the following charms underneath your pillow: a petticoat or garter worn by a bride on her wedding day, an onion, daisy roots, a piece of wedding cake wrapped in white satin and lace, a poplar branch tied to your stockings or socks, or two laurel leaves picked by a Witch on Saint Valentine's Day.

5. Before going to sleep, bathe in bathwater containing some lavender oil and rosewater, and then rub your temples with three drops of blood from a white dove. (IMPORTANT NOTE: The best way to obtain the dove's blood is to find a dove that is already dead. Never kill a live dove! If you do, bad luck will surely come your way. Most Wiccans and modern-day Pagans agree that the deliberate taking of any life is unnecessary for modern white magick and is in violation of the Wiccan Rede.)

6. Another lover's dream-spell requiring blood from a dove comes from a medieval treatise on oneiromancy (the art and practice of dream interpretation): Mix together

magnet dust and powdered coral with the blood of a white dove to form a dough. Enclose it in a large fig, wrap it in a piece of blue cloth, and then wear it on a gold chain around your neck as you sleep.

HERBAL LOVE POTIONS: Add to wine or food any of the following herbs to make a powerful love potion—balm, basil, powdered cardamom seeds, carrot root, cinnamon, cumin, dill seed, dittany of Crete, fennel seeds, grains of paradise, marjoram, powdered orris root, parsley.

ORANGE SPELL: To gain the affections of a certain person, write his or her full name and birthdate on the inside of a dried, heart-shaped orange peel. Burn it along with dried orange blossoms as you concentrate upon your beloved and chant his or her name out loud. Gather the ashes and keep them in a sealed Witch Bottle.

PASSION SPELL: To make your man more passionate in bed, write his name on a red phallus-shaped candle (available at most occult shops), stroke it nine times with musk oil, and then pass it through the smoke of musk incense. Light the candle once a day, letting it burn down only half an inch each time. When the candle is finished, wrap it in a piece of red satin and keep it under your bed for a whole month.

WITCH BOTTLE LOVE SPELL: To win the affections of a certain lady or gentleman, perform this spell when the Moon is in the astrological sign of Taurus, or on any Friday night when the Moon is in a waxing phase.

Mix a handful of quassia chips with some hair and/or fingernail clippings from your beloved, and burn to ashes. Mix the ashes with some dried rose petals and place in a small bottle. After sealing the bottle, tape a photograph of your beloved or a piece of fabric taken from his or her clothing to it. Wrap a square piece of new pink satin around the bottle and tie it securely with a pink or white ribbon. Anoint the satin-covered bottle with two drops of rose oil or mint oil, and then pass it through the smoke of jasmine-scented incense as you chant out loud the name of the person from whom you desire love, willing him or her to desire you, until the incense burns itself completely out.

To Reverse This Spell: When the Moon is in a waning phase, remove the ribbon and satin from the bottle and burn them. Open the bottle and pour its contents out into a moving body of water as you say thrice: "Love's direction now has shifted. Let this lover's spell be lifted!" Break the Witch Bottle with a rock (taking care not to get glass in your eyes) and then carefully bury the broken pieces in the ground.

To Reunite Parted Lovers

When the Moon is in a waxing phase, prick the tip of your left index finger with a sterilized pin or needle, and squeeze out a bit of blood.

Use the blood to write your initials on a smooth white stone as you visualize being back together with your lover. Write his or her initials next to yours and then draw three circles of blood around both initials.

Wrap the stone in a piece of pink or red velvet tied with a pink ribbon, and then bury it in the ground or in a flowerpot in which any Venus-ruled herb or flower is growing.

If the spell is done correctly, you and your lover should be reunited within a period of three days and nights.

Aphrodisiacs

GINSENG APHRODISIAC—Ginseng is considered to be the ultimate aphrodisiac by many around the world. The best preparation of ginseng to use is any liquid tonic that has the root in the bottle with it. (Several brands can be found in many health food stores, occult supply shops, mail order herb suppliers, and in local herb shops in any metropolitan Chinatown district.)

To increase the sex drive, light a red phallus-shaped candle, burn musk incense on an altar dedicated to Lakshmi (the Hindu goddess of sexual pleasures), and drink four fluid ounces of the ginseng tonic two times daily for at least one week before engaging in sexual activity with your lover.

TO CURE MALE IMPOTENCE AND FEMALE FRIGIDITY— Drink two cups of the following potion before turning in for the night and apply some of it to the base of your lower spine as well:

By the light of a red candle, bring one quart of water (preferably clear rainwater or mountain spring water) to a boil in your cauldron. Add 3½ tablespoons of fenugreek seed, cover and simmer for five minutes. Remove from heat, add two handfuls of savory, and then steep for about an hour before using.

PASSION POTION FOR LOVERS—For more passionate love-making or to overcome sexual frigidity, concoct the following passion potion for yourself and/or your lover. (It doesn't taste all that great, but it's quite safe, easy to prepare, and *very* effective!)

By the light of a red candle, bring one quart of water (preferably clear rainwater or mountain spring water) to a boil in your cauldron. Remove from heat and add two cups of coarsely chopped fresh parsley herb. Cover the cauldron and allow the potion to steep for an hour.

Drink two cups of the passion potion at least twenty minutes before making love with your partner. (And be sure that it's very warm when you drink it.)

SOUTH AMERICAN APHRODISIAC—Steep four to six dried vanilla pods in two cups of tequila or imported cognac for three weeks in a tightly sealed glass bottle, shaking it several times daily.

Take ten to twenty drops, two or three times a day, to stimulate the sex drive and to make lovemaking more passionate.

FERTILITY POTION (FOR MEN AND WOMEN)—To overcome infertility, increase sperm count, and strengthen the sex drive, burn one stick of musk incense as an offering to the fertility deity of your choice, and take twenty milligrams of royal jelly every day. (Not only does royal jelly possess sexual rejuvenating properties, it is also reputed to increase the size of the male genitals if used often enough!)

MALE POTENCY SPELL To magickally boost a weakened sex drive in men, or to help cure male impotence, perform this spell on a night when the Moon is in the astrological sign of Scorpio.

Take seven keys from seven houses in seven towns and place them in a blazing fire until they glow red-hot. Then pour cold water gathered from seven wells over the hot keys and as you expose your private parts to the rising steam, repeat the following magickal incantation seven times:

> SEVEN KEYS AND SEVEN SONGS
> RENEW MY MANHOOD
> TWICE AS STRONG

Spell to Win Court Cases

When the Moon is in the astrological sign of Libra or Sagittarius, brew a magickal tea from a lovage root. Strain the liquid into a glass container (such as a small jelly jar). Seal it tightly with a lid after the tea has cooled down; bless it in the divine name of the Goddess; and then store it in the refrigerator until the night before you are scheduled to appear in court.

When the time is ready, light a new black candle and add the lovage root tea to your bathwater. As you bathe in it and visualize yourself winning the court case, your body and spirit will absorb beneficial occult vibrations.

After bathing, place the Justice card from a Tarot deck under your pillow. Go to bed and recite the following magickal rhyme over and over (either to yourself or out loud) until you fall asleep:

SCALES OF JUSTICE, HARKEN AND QUAVER;
LET THE JUDGE RULE IN MY FAVOR.

To make the power of the spell even more potent, also brew a magickal tea from some dried California buckthorn bark and sprinkle it around the courthouse premises at midnight on the night prior to your court appearance. Be sure to do this without anybody seeing you.

Magick for Diviners

SPIRIT AID—To gain the help of benevolent entities when performing any divinatory art, mix together wild thyme and wood sorrel and burn the mixture as an incense offering to the spirit world.

TO INCREASE PSYCHIC VISION—Burn some dried mugwort as a magickal incense while scrying (crystal ball gazing). Brewed as a tea, often with lemon balm, mugwort can be consumed to aid divination, meditation, and all forms of psychic development. Many Witches and scryers use mugwort tea also as a wash to cleanse and consecrate crystal balls, magick mirrors, and other objects used in the ancient occult art of scrying.

SPIRITUAL POWER SPELL—To increase your spiritual mediumistic powers, mix cloves with some dried and ground chicory root and cinquefoil. Burn as an incense offering to the spirit world when conducting seances or consulting a Ouija board.

A Spell for Poetic Inspiration

Light a purple candle. Clear your mind of all distractions and negative thoughts, and then recite the following invocations until you feel inspired:

O GREAT APOLLO: OLYMPIAN LORD OF POETRY AND MUSIC, I CALL UPON THEE AND ASK THEE NOW TO BLESS MY SOUL, HEART AND MIND WITH YOUR DIVINE INSPIRATION. LET YOUR POWERFUL MUSE GUIDE ME IN ALL THAT I DO. SO MOTE IT BE.

O GREAT GOD WODEN: MASTER OF INSPIRED PSYCHIC ACTIVITY AND GOD OF SKALD-CRAFT, I CALL UPON THEE AND ASK THEE NOW TO BLESS MY SOUL, HEART AND MIND WITH YOUR DIVINE INSPIRATION. LET YOUR POWERFUL MUSE GUIDE ME IN ALL THAT I DO. SO MOTE IT BE.

SWEET LADY BRIGIT: ANCIENT GODDESS OF FIRE, AND PATRONESS OF ALL POETS, I CALL UPON THEE AND ASK THEE NOW TO BLESS MY SOUL, HEART AND MIND WITH YOUR DIVINE INSPIRATION. LET YOUR POWERFUL MUSE GUIDE ME IN ALL THAT I DO. SO MOTE IT BE.

O GREAT LORD BRAGI: BEARDED GOD OF POETRY AND SONG, I CALL UPON THEE AND ASK THEE NOW TO BLESS MY SOUL, HEART AND MIND WITH YOUR DIVINE INSPIRATION. LET YOUR POWERFUL MUSE GUIDE ME IN ALL THAT I DO. SO MOTE IT BE.

In addition to the Pagan deities who govern the art of poetry, you may also call upon the ancient Greek Muses as a source of poetic inspiration.

Although the Muses as a group preside over all forms of poetry (as well as the art of music), each of the nine rule a specific field of interest. The individual Muses and their most accepted provinces are as follows: *CALLIOPE* (epic or heroic poetry); *CLIO* (historical verse); *ERATO* (love poems, hymns, and lyric poetry); *EUTERPE* (tragedy, lyric poetry, and music); *MELPOMENE* (tragedy); *POLYHYMNIA* (hymns, song, and prose); *TERPSICHORE* (dance and song); *THALIA* (comedy and pastoral poetry); and *URANIA* (cosmological poetry).

IMPORTANT NOTE: Although you may invoke the Gods and/or the Muses at any time when inspiration is needed, this particular spell seems to work best when it is performed on a Wednesday (the proper day of the week to perform spells and rituals involving all forms of writing). And, of course, don't forget to always thank the Gods for their precious gifts.

Good Luck Herb Jar

To attract good fortune into your life or to change a streak of bad luck to good, fill a jar with any combination of the following magickal herbs: buckthorn bark, chamomile, clover, dandelion, frankincense, heal-all, honeysuckle, huckleberry leaves, Irish moss, Job's tears, John the Conqueror, khus-khus, lotus, lucky hand root, mistletoe, mojo wish bean, myrrh, nutmeg, peony root, queen of the meadow, rose hips, rosemary, sacred bark, sandalwood, spearmint, star anise, thyme, tonka bean.

Seal the jar tightly and keep it in your kitchen on a shelf or on a windowsill. Place your hands upon the jar each morning after you wake up, and say:

> TO GOD AND GODDESS I DO PRAY
> GUIDE ME THROUGH ANOTHER DAY
> LET GOOD FORTUNE COME MY WAY
> GOOD LUCK HITHER NOW I SAY

After reciting the magickal incantation, gently shake the jar a few times and then kiss it before putting it back.

Gaia Healing Spell

To send out positive "healing" vibrations to the planet, perform this spell during an eclipse or when the Moon is in a waxing phase.

Arrange seashells on a secluded beach to form a magick circle at least five feet in diameter. (If you do not have access to a beach, you may perform this spell in a forest or secluded garden using stones, branches and/or flowers to form the circle.)

Kneel in the center of the circle, facing the ocean. Light a blue candle and a stick of incense and place them before you. Raise your arms high with palms up in a traditional Witch's prayer position, and recite the following chant:

WITH SMOKE AND FLAME
THIS SPELL'S BEGUN.
O GODDESS OF THE STARS,
MOON AND THE SUN,
LET THE HEALING POWER BEGIN.
LET THE EARTH BE WHOLE AGAIN.

THE EARTH IS MY MOTHER
AND I AM HER CHILD.
THE EARTH IS MY LOVER
FREE AND WILD.
HEAL ON THE OUTSIDE; HEAL WITHIN,
LAND AND SEA, FIRE AND WIND.

WITH LOVE SINCERE I CHANT THIS PRAYER
TO MAKE MANKIND BEGIN TO CARE.
LET EVERY SISTER AND EVERY BROTHER
HEAL THE WOUNDS OF THE GREAT EARTH MOTHER.

LET THE HEALING POWER BEGIN,
LET THE EARTH BE WHOLE AGAIN.
HEAL ON THE OUTSIDE; HEAL WITHIN,
LAND AND SEA, FIRE AND WIND.

SO MOTE IT BE!

Money Spells

1. To attract money and good fortune, burn a bayberry-scented candle and sprinkle some dried and powdered bayberry root in the candle's flame.

2. Brew a tea from the herb known as earth-smoke and sprinkle it all around the inside and outside of your home, as well as on the bottom of your shoes.

3. Soak khus-khus in rainwater for at least three days. Strain the liquid into a bottle and add it to your bathwater. Khus-khus can also be carried in a red flannel mojo bag to attract wealth, success, and good luck into your life.

4. Make a money-drawing Witch Bottle: By the light of a green candle, put a bayberry root, a lucky hand root, a mandrake root, and a snake root into a small jar. Fill the jar to the top with tea made from spikenard. Cap the jar tightly and pour a bit of melted wax from the green candle onto the lid to charge it with money-drawing magickal energy.

Gambler's Charm

Take a devil's shoestring (one of the most popular roots used magickally in the Voodoo religion) and cut it into small pieces. Put them in a jar and fill it to the top with whiskey and camphor. Seal the jar tightly and anoint it once a week with three drops of lavender oil.

Before gambling, take a piece of root out of the jar and rub it between your hands while commanding it to bring you good luck.

Carry it in your purse or pocket as a good luck/money-drawing charm when you gamble, and return it to the jar after you have collected your winnings.

You must have the utmost faith in both the power of the devil's shoestring and in yourself or else the root will not work its magick for you.

Wish-Magick

With the exception of love-magick, wish-magick is perhaps the most popular form of white magick practiced in modern times. It is relatively easy to perform, and can be as simple as wishing on a star, breaking a wishbone, or dropping a coin into a fountain or wishing well.

Many magickally minded folks firmly believe in the power of the seven-knob candle (or "wish-candle" as it is sometimes called) to make wishes come true. It is a magickal tool especially popular among practitioners of hoodoo folk magick in the southern regions of the United States. Seven-knob candles are easily obtainable in most occult supply shops (see the Pagan Resources Chapter at the end of this book) and are available in a variety of colors. When used correctly, they can work powerful magick, but be careful what you wish for, as the old expression goes, because you just might get it!

To perform the following wishing spell, you will need a blue seven-knob candle, myrrh oil, and a consecrated athame.

Write your wish on each of the seven knobs of the candle. Anoint the candle with the myrrh oil and say:

> I CONSECRATE AND BLESS THIS CANDLE
> IN THE DIVINE NAME OF THE GODDESS.
> LET ALL NEGATIVITY AND HINDRANCE
> BE CAST FORTH HENCEFROM.

Pick up your athame with your right hand. Place the flat side of the blade on top of the candle and envision magickal energy as a white light flowing from your body through the athame and into the candle. When you begin to actually feel the energy flowing, say:

I CHARGE THEE NOW
WITH MAGICKAL POWER
IN THE DIVINE NAME OF THE GODDESS.

Charge the candle for at least five minutes, return the athame to the altar, and then light the top knob of the wish-candle. Say the following incantation seven times:

SEVEN MAGICK KNOBS OF BLUE
MAKE THIS WISH OF MINE COME TRUE.

As the candle burns, concentrate upon the thing you desire and visualize yourself already in possession of it.

Extinguish the candle after the first knob has burned down, and repeat the entire spell for the next six nights in a row, burning only one knob of the candle each time.

Spell to Weaken a Sorcerer's Power

On the first night of a waning Moon, scorch a lucky rabbit's foot with the flame of a consecrated black candle and then place the charm on a square piece of brand-new black cloth. Sprinkle it with a mixture of graveyard dirt and guinea pepper, and then place on top of it, face down, a photograph (or drawing) of the sorcerer who is using negative power against you. (You can also use a piece of parchment paper upon which you have written the sorcerer's true name backward in dragon's blood ink, which can be obtained at most occult shops or through mail-order occult catalogues.) Wrap the amulet in the black cloth, being sure to make each fold away from you (never toward you), and then tie it securely with a piece of black yarn.

Bore a hole in the western side of a tree on the sorcerer's property (or as close to his or her home as possible) and then hide the amulet inside the hole. As the sun sets each evening, the sorcerer's power over you will grow weaker and weaker.

Spells to Deal With an Enemy

Unfortunately, in many people's lives there is at least one man or woman who, for one reason or another, falls under the classification of an enemy: a jealous rival, a bitter ex-spouse, or a neighbor from hell, just to name a few examples.

Sometimes enemies can be most difficult, if not impossible, to deal with, and one must turn to magick when all else fails. There is nothing wrong with using magick on your enemies 'as long as the magick is of a white or positive nature, but many practitioners of the magickal arts, especially novices, make the mistake of trying to use black magick or sorcery to take revenge on their foes.

Before turning to the supernatural aid of hexes, dangerous curses that can backfire, Voodoo dolls, or Satanic mumbo jumbo to get even, you should keep in mind that any form of black magick is a major violation of the Wiccan Rede. You should also remember that it is terribly self-destructive, as the casting of such negative spells only results in threefold negativity instantly returned upon the sender, which is you. Therefore, no matter how strong your anger is for another person, or what he or she has done to infuriate you, you should *never* resort to the use of black magick or sorcery.

This is not to say that we Witches must sit idly by and allow an adversary to continue making our lives totally unbearable. The good news is that there are many positive ways one may magickally deal with an enemy without violating the Wiccan Rede, as the following spells demonstrate:

TO PREVENT PSYCHIC ATTACK BY ENEMIES—Psychic attacks usually occur at night when we are sleeping and our minds are in a vulnerable state. If you feel that an enemy is attempting to use psychic energies to cause you to have nightmares, misfortune, and/or ill health, do the following before going to bed: Draw an invisible circle of protection around your bed with a consecrated athame, place white votive candles in glass holders near each corner of your bed, burn asafetida in an incense burner in your bedroom, and visualize yourself surrounded by a white impenetrable ring of magickal light as you lie in bed waiting to fall asleep. A red charm bag filled with witch grass or asafetida also helps ward off psychic attacks (as well as all forms of negativity) when hung over the bed. Another method of protection is to sleep with protective gemstones (such as cat's eye or sapphire) or other amulets of protection under and around your bed. (To find which amulets are right for you, see Chapter Two—AMULET POWER.)

TO HELP CHANGE ENEMIES INTO FRIENDS—Take a photograph of your enemy and pass it through the rising smoke of jasmine, orange, vanilla, or violet incense. As you do this, recite the following incantation thrice:

> ENEMY, ENEMY, TURN INTO FRIEND,
> LET ALL ILL WILL NOW COME TO AN END.

(If you do not have a photograph of your enemy, you can use a square piece of blue parchment paper upon which you have written his or her full name and birthdate, if known.)

After reciting the incantation for the third time, take the photograph or blue parchment and put it in a small box along with a beryl gemstone. Fill the box with vervain, cover it with a lid, and then store it in an undisturbed place.

For best results, perform this spell when the Moon is full.

TO STOP AN ENEMY FROM SPREADING GOSSIP ABOUT YOU—Write the name and full birthdate of your gossiping enemy on a piece of slippery elm bark. Wrap it in a piece of black cloth and say:

> (Name of enemy) BE NOW SILENT,
> LET YOUR BITTER TONGUE BE BROKEN.
> (Name of enemy) BE NOW SILENT,
> LET NO EVIL WORDS BE SPOKEN.
> SO MOTE IT BE!

Bury the cloth-covered bark in a forest or graveyard at night by the light of a pale waning moon as you visualize your enemy unable to speak whenever he or she attempts to spread malicious gossip about you.

TO MAKE AN ENEMY MOVE—When the Moon is in a waning phase, write on white parchment the full name of the person you want to move away from you, along with his or her complete birthdate (if know).

Roll up the paper along with a photograph of the enemy (if you happen to have one handy), place them inside a bottle of vinegar, and then toss it into a moving body of water as you visualize your enemy moving far away and never bothering you again.

This is an ideal spell to use when all else seems to fail.

The Evil Eye

An old spell to avert the powers of the evil eye called for nine toads to be strung alive on the same string, and then buried at midnight in hallowed ground.

A more modern (and less gross) method to counteract the evil eye is as follows: Using a consecrated athame, cut a small piece of rowan wood (mountain ash) on Saint John's Day, Samhain, or on any night when the Moon is in a waxing phase. Paint the ancient Egyptian symbol of the Eye of Horus on the wood with blue paint. (Since ancient times, blue has been used as an evil eye averting color.) After the paint dries, carry the piece of rowan wood as a protective amulet in your pocket, purse, or mojo charm bag.

Other magickal methods to protect yourself against the evil eye include sleeping with a string of nine knots underneath your pillow, and the act of turning yourself completely around seven times in a clockwise direction.

The latter method also works well for breaking a streak of bad luck, especially if performed during the waning phase of the Moon as the following incantation is recited upon each turn:

> OMENS ILL AND DEVIL'S BANE,
> DECREASE AND THEN CEASE
> AS THE DARK MOON WANES.

To Keep Evil From Your House

Make a magickal tea from any of the following herbs and then sprinkle some of it in the corners and doorways of your home to purify, defeat all wicked conjuring, and prevent evil forces from entering: angelica root, broom tops, curry powder, holy thistle, poke root (which can also be added to your bath or cleaning water), and tormentil.

Exorcism Spell

To purify any place of all evil entities or any supernatural force of a negative nature, take some dried and powdered sloe bark and mix it with any strong unhexing oil (available in most occult shops), garlic powder, and frankincense.

With a new white candle lit, burn the mixture in a fireproof dish at the stroke of midday and at the stroke of midnight in the area of negativity.

Repeat the exorcism for seven days in a row.

Unhexing Spells

HEX-BREAKING—(1) To break the power of any hex that another has inflicted upon you, burn any of the following dried herbs upon a hot charcoal block as a powerful hex-breaking incense: African ginger, agrimony, ague (root or weed), ash tree leaves, benzoin, betony, Chewing John root, pine tree needles, vervain (especially when mixed with dill, Saint John's wort, and trefoil), and vendal root.

These herbs will not only work well to remove the hex or crossing, they will also send the evil back to the person who has hexed you.

(2) To remove the hex from a child who has been victimized by sorcery, have the child stand on his or her head and count backward, starting from number ninety-nine. By the time the child reaches number one, the hex will have been broken. (If any of the numbers are accidentally left out or counted down in the wrong order, the spell must then be repeated from the beginning or it will not work.)

(3) Another method to remove a hex is to chew a piece of Low John the Conqueror root, spit it out onto the ground, and then say thrice:

> GONE BE NOW THIS HEX,
> BROKEN BE THIS CURSE,
> LET THE EVIL POWER
> THREEFOLD BE REVERSED!

A SPELL FOR UNHEXING YOUR HOME—To break the evil power of hexes and curses placed upon your home, mix some nettle herb (dried) with any strong jinx or hex-breaking powder (available in nearly all occult shops and mail-order Witchcraft catalogues), and then sprinkle some of it in the corners of each room of your house and outside every door and window. (This spell can also be used for removing hexes from offices, barns, and other buildings as well.)

TO BREAK A VOODOO CURSE—On a night when the Moon is in a waning phase, take a blood root (a favorite Voodoo root used for breaking all evil spells and hexes) and throw it onto the doorstep of the person who has placed the curse upon you. You will then be released from his or her magickal power and the imprecation will immediately be turned back to the sender of the curse.

TO BREAK A SORCERER'S CURSE—If you feel that a sorcerer or sorceress has placed a magickal curse upon you, your home, or your family, perform this curse-breaking spell just before midnight on the last night of the full Moon.

Light a new white candle and burn any of the following incense in a fireproof container: cloves, frankincense, hyacinth, lilac, pine, or sage.

Hold a lucky rabbit's-foot charm over your heart and repeat the following incantation thirteen times:

> WITH RABBIT'S FOOT AND MAGICK VERSE
> I TURN AROUND THIS WICKED CURSE.
> AS THESE WORDS OF MINE ARE SPOKEN
> LET THIS EVIL SPELL BE BROKEN.

Repeat this spell nightly (using a brand-new candle each time) until the phase of the New Moon.

Wrap the leftover wax from the candles in a white piece of cotton and then bury it in the ground in a secret spot where it will remain undisturbed.

Healing Spells

QUARTZ CRYSTAL SPELL—To help cure many illnesses, perform this ancient spell from England: Gather nine quartz crystals (also known as "star-stones") from a running brook. Fill a cauldron with a quart of clear water from the same brook, add the quartz crystals, and then bring to a boil for nine minutes to transfer the curative properties of the crystals to the water. Drink some of the water each morning for nine consecutive days. This should help speed your recovery.

HEX CURE—To cure a human or beast who has been made ill by the powers of a hex, according to traiteurs (hex-doctors) of the southeastern region of the United States, brew a tea from the wahoo bark, rub it gently on the forehead of the afflicted person or animal, and then say the word "wahoo" seven times.

TO PROLONG LIFE—Brew a tea from the herb known as "life everlasting" and before you drink it, repeat these ancient magickal words:

> CHILLS AND ILLS
> PAINS AND BANES
> DO YOUR FASTING
> AND LIFE EVERLASTING.

A MODERN WITCH'S HEALING SPELL—To help speed a recovery from illness, write the sick person's name upon a white human-shaped candle of the appropriate gender. As you anoint it with three drops of myrrh or mint oil, visualize healing energy in the form of white light flowing from your hands into the candle, and say:

IN THE DIVINE NAME OF THE GODDESS
WHO BREATHES LIFE INTO US ALL
I CONSECRATE AND CHARGE THIS CANDLE
AS A MAGICKAL TOOL FOR HEALING.

Place the candle on top of a photograph of the sick person and then light the wick. As the candle burns down, concentrate upon the person in the photograph, willing him or her to be well again, and chant the following incantation:

MAGICK MEND AND CANDLE BURN,
SICKNESS END; GOOD HEALTH RETURN.

HEADACHE CURING SPELL—In ancient Egypt, healers and practitioners of the magickal arts cured headaches (and other bodily aches and pains) in the following manner: First, a nail would be rubbed on the part of the body where the pain was, and then either placed under the patient's pillow for a night in order to absorb the pain while he or she slept, or nailed into a tree, a town gate, or a special pillar.

WART CURING SPELL—In days of old, before wart-removing medicines were invented, sympathetic magick was commonly employed by Witches and folk-healers for the curing of warts.

The most popular method was to rub something on the wart (such as a clove of garlic, an onion, an apple slice, a bean, or a piece of meat) and then bury it in the ground at night during the waning phase of the Moon. This was done in the belief that as the buried object rotted away, it would magickally cause the wart to disappear (usually within nine days).

JAUNDICE CURING SPELL—To cure yourself of jaundice, according to an old grimoire of Cuban witchcraft, string together thirteen fresh cloves of garlic on a white cord. Knot the two ends together and wear the string of garlic as an amuletic necklace for thirteen days and thirteen nights.

At the stroke of midnight on the final night, remove the string of garlic while standing in the middle of a crossroad and toss it over your left shoulder. Without looking behind you (not even once), quickly return home and go straight to bed.

Spell to Help Sell a House

When the Moon is in the astrological sign of Taurus, light a new green candle (preferably a pine-scented one) and then anoint a small Saint Joseph statue with three drops of pine oil. (Saint Joseph statues can be obtained at most stores that specialize in religious goods, and the inexpensive plastic ones work just as well as the expensive marble ones.)

Light a stick or cone of pine incense and place it in a fireproof incense burner. Pass the statue through the aromatic rising smoke and say thrice:

> SMOKE OF PINE AND WITCH'S FIRE
> BRING TO MY HOUSE A QUALIFIED BUYER
> LET THE SALE BE QUICK AND FAIR
> O SAINT JOSEPH, PLEASE ANSWER MY PRAYER.

As you recite the magickal rhyme, focus your thoughts and energies upon the house you wish to sell and visualize it already sold. (For instance, imagine a "sold" sign in the front yard or seeing yourself and your family moving your possessions out of the house and into a moving van.)

Dig a small hole in the front yard and put the Saint Joseph statue in it upside down and facing the house. (If you do not have a front yard, you can bury the statue in a flowerpot near the front door of your home and the spell will work just as well.)

It is traditional to leave the buried statue behind when you move away in order to bring good luck and spiritual protection to the new occupants of the house. If you choose not to leave the statue behind, however, be sure not to dig it up until after the final closing of the real estate transaction, otherwise you might reverse the positive effects of the spell.

This particular spell helped me sell my own house a few years back. I know of quite a few people (and they aren't even Witches!) who strongly believe in the house-selling magickal power of the Saint Joseph statue.

Wiccaning

The Wiccaning Ritual is a Wiccan birth rite by which a newborn baby is given a legal name and/or a Craft name (also known as an "eke-name") by his or her parents, and then spiritually "purified" and blessed in the divine name of the Goddess. In some ways it is like a modern Witch's version of the Christian baptismal ceremony.

The rite is traditionally performed by the High Priestess of a coven, but there is no reason why a Solitary Witch cannot perform it as well.

It should take place during a waxing or full moon (never during a waning one) and preferably when the lunar position corresponds with the child's astrological sign. For instance: When the waxing or full moon is in Taurus or in any of the other earth signs, it is the ideal time to perform a Wiccaning for a child born under the sign of Taurus the bull.

The following is a detailed ritual outline for a Wiccaning:

The Rite of Wiccaning

Erect an altar, facing north. Around it, cast a circle about nine feet in diameter.

In the center of the altar, place a small candle upon which the child's full birthdate, astrological symbol, and new name have been written. (Use a pink candle for a baby girl, a blue candle for a baby boy.) To the right of the candle (East), place a large censer of frankincense and myrrh, and a consecrated athame. To the left of the candle (West), place a goblet of water (preferably fresh rainwater, if at all possible) and an altar bell. Behind the candle (North), place a small dish of salt. To the right of the altar, place a chair or cushion for the mother to sit on while she holds the baby in her arms.

Light four white votive candles and place them clockwise along the circumference of the circle (the first one at the eastern quadrant, the second one at the southern quadrant, the third one at the western quadrant, and the fourth one at the northern quadrant behind the altar.)

Ring the altar bell thrice. Take the athame in your right hand, point it straight up to the sky, and say:

> HARKEN WELL YE ELEMENTS
> OF AIR, FIRE, WATER, AND EARTH,
> BY BELL AND BLADE I SUMMON THEE
> ON THIS SACRED NIGHT OF MIRTH.

Turn to the east. Lower your right arm so that the tip of the athame is pointing to the candle at the eastern quadrant of the circle and say:

> I SUMMON THEE NOW
> O SACRED SYLPHS OF THE AIR
> AND ELEMENTAL KINGS OF THE EAST
> TO WITNESS THIS HOLIEST OF RITES
> AND TO PROTECT THIS WICCAN CIRCLE.

Turn to the south. Point the tip of the athame to the candle at the southern quadrant of the circle and say:

> I SUMMON THEE NOW
> O SACRED SALAMANDERS OF THE FIRE
> AND ELEMENTAL KINGS OF THE SOUTH
> TO WITNESS THIS HOLIEST OF RITES
> AND TO PROTECT THIS WICCAN CIRCLE.

Turn to the west. Point the tip of the athame to the candle at the western quadrant of the circle and say:

> I SUMMON THEE NOW
> O SACRED UNDINES OF THE WATER
> AND ELEMENTAL KINGS OF THE WEST
> TO WITNESS THIS HOLIEST OF RITES
> AND TO PROTECT THIS WICCAN CIRCLE.

Turn to the north. Point the tip of the athame to the candle at the northern quadrant of the circle and say:

> I SUMMON THEE NOW
> O SACRED GNOMES OF THE EARTH
> AND ELEMENTAL KINGS OF THE NORTH
> TO WITNESS THIS HOLIEST OF RITES
> AND TO PROTECT THIS WICCAN CIRCLE.

Return to the altar.

Using the athame, draw an invisible pentagram symbol in the air over the dish of salt. Put down the athame and then pour all of the salt into the goblet of water. Stir with the blade of the athame until the salt is completely dissolved, and as you do this, recite the following incantation:

> WITH THIS SACRED SALT
> I CONSECRATE THIS GOBLET OF WATER.
> LET ALL EVIL SPIRITS
> BE CAST FORTH HENCEFROM!
> LET ALL NEGATIVE VIBRATIONS
> BE CAST FORTH HENCEFROM!
> LET ALL IMPURITIES AND HINDRANCES
> BE CAST FORTH HENCEFROM!
> BLESSED BE THIS GOBLET OF WATER
> IN THE DIVINE NAME OF THE GODDESS
> AND IN THE NAME OF HER CONSORT
> THE GREAT HORNED GOD.

Return the athame to the right side of the altar. Take the goblet of water in your left hand and stand before the mother and her baby. The mother should now stand, holding the child so that he or she faces you.

Dip the index finger of your right hand into the water. Anoint the child with the saltwater mixture by making the sacred symbol of the pentagram on the child's forehead with your finger, and then say:

> BLESSED BE THIS CHILD OF THE GODDESS!

All coveners present should now say in unison:

> BLESSED BE THIS CHILD OF THE GODDESS!

Dip your right index finger into the goblet of water once again. Use your finger to anoint the child by making the sacred symbol of the pentagram, this time on the child's chest.

After the child has been anointed, recite the following Wiccan prayer:

MAY YOUR HEART BE BLESSED WITH LOVE,
MAY YOUR MIND BE BLESSED WITH WISDOM,
MAY YOUR SOUL BE BLESSED WITH MAGICK,
MAY YOUR LIFE BE JOYOUS AND LONG
AND BLESSED WITH PEACE
FREEDOM AND CONTENTMENT
AND ALL THAT IS GOOD.
BLESSED BE THIS CHILD OF THE GODDESS!

All coveners present should now say in unison:

BLESSED BE THIS CHILD OF THE GODDESS!

The mother should now move to the center of the circle with the child and say:

IN THIS CONSECRATED CIRCLE
OF WICCAN LOVE AND WICCAN LIGHT
SHALL THIS BEAUTIFUL CHILD OF THE GODDESS
BE GIVEN THE NAME...(NAME OF CHILD)
BLESSED BE...(NAME OF CHILD)

All coveners present should now say in unison:

BLESSED BE...(NAME OF CHILD)

Light the censer of frankincense and myrrh, and place it on the ground in the center of the circle.

The mother should now pass the child through the rising smoke of the incense three times as a gesture of spiritual purification as you say:

MAY THE GODDESS AND THE HORNED GOD
BLESS YOU, GUIDE YOU, AND PROTECT YOU
IN ALL THAT YOU DO
FOR AS LONG AS YOU SHALL LIVE.
SO MOTE IT BE!

All coveners present should now say in unison:

SO MOTE IT BE!

The mother and baby should now return to the seat next to the altar.

It is now time to uncast the circle and end the Rite of Wiccaning.

Take the athame in your left hand and point the tip of it to the candle at the northern quadrant of the circle, and say:

O SACRED GNOMES OF THE EARTH
AND ELEMENTAL KINGS OF THE NORTH
WE OFFER THEE OUR DEEPEST THANKS
FOR YOUR PRESENCE AND PROTECTION
DURING THIS SACRED RITE OF WICCANING.
I NOW RELEASE THEE FROM THIS CIRCLE
AND BID THEE FAREWELL.

Turn to the west. Point the tip of the athame to the candle at the western quadrant of the circle and say:

O SACRED UNDINES OF THE WATER
AND ELEMENTAL KINGS OF THE WEST
WE OFFER THEE OUR DEEPEST THANKS
FOR YOUR PRESENCE AND PROTECTION
DURING THIS SACRED RITE OF WICCANING.
I NOW RELEASE THEE FROM THIS CIRCLE
AND BID THEE FAREWELL.

Turn to the south. Point the tip of the athame to the candle at the southern quadrant of the circle and say:

> O SACRED SALAMANDERS OF THE FIRE
> AND ELEMENTAL KINGS OF THE SOUTH
> WE OFFER THEE OUR DEEPEST THANKS
> FOR YOUR PRESENCE AND PROTECTION
> DURING THIS SACRED RITE OF WICCANING.
> I NOW RELEASE THEE FROM THIS CIRCLE
> AND BID THEE FAREWELL.

Turn to the east. Point the tip of the athame to the candle at the eastern quadrant of the circle and say:

> O SACRED SYLPHS OF THE AIR
> AND ELEMENTAL KINGS OF THE EAST
> WE OFFER THEE OUR DEEPEST THANKS
> FOR YOUR PRESENCE AND PROTECTION
> DURING THIS SACRED RITE OF WICCANING.
> I NOW RELEASE THEE FROM THIS CIRCLE
> AND BID THEE FAREWELL.

Return the athame to its place on the altar. Give thanks, in your own words, to the Goddess and the Horned God, and then say:

> THIS CIRCLE IS NOW UNCAST.
> THIS RITE IS NOW ENDED.
> SO MOTE IT BE!

Ring the altar bell three times, and say:

> MERRY MEET AND MERRY PART
> AND MERRY MEET AGAIN.

Although the Wiccaning Rite is officially over, many covens like to end the evening with a traditional "Cakes and Ale" or "Cakes and Wine" ceremony.

2

Amulet Power

Acorn

An acorn anointed with musk oil and carried in your purse, pocket, or charm bag will help to attract the opposite sex to you. To increase your income, anoint an acorn with three drops of pine oil when the Moon is waxing, and then bury it in your yard as close as possible to the front door of your house. For Witches and Pagans who follow a Druidic or Celtic tradition, three acorns placed on a Yule Sabbat altar will help increase magickal or divinatory powers and also bring peace and protection to a Druid circle. At one time, acorns were commonly used by practitioners of the occult arts as an amulet to gain immortality.

Adam and Eve Root

Carry a musk or rose oil-anointed Adam and Eve root in your pocket, purse, or charm bag as an amulet to attract the opposite sex or to make any form of love magick more potent.

Agate

Agate is a semiprecious crystalline gemstone that attracts good luck, aids meditation, and protects against accidental falls and all kinds of danger. It is the symbol of health and long life, and a powerful good luck charm for all persons born in the month of June. Witches have long used this gemstone in rituals to invoke the powers of the Goddess and the Horned God. According to medieval belief, an agate amulet can reduce fever, relieve thirst (when placed in the mouth), and protect against the bites of scorpions and serpents. To purify the blood, according to Arabian legend, wear an agate amulet in the shape of an arrow.

Aladdin's Lamp

Wear a gold charm in the shape of an Aladdin's lamp in order to bring you good luck and happiness in all that you do. Rub the lamp amulet to make wishes and dreams come true.

Alligator Teeth

To protect yourself against all forms of sorcery, wear a necklace made of alligator teeth around your neck. In various folklores, alligator teeth are also believed to possess the power to heal the body and to counteract poison.

Amber

Amber is a good-luck gemstone that strengthens the aura, and harmonizes and balances the yin/yang energies. It attracts compassion and can be worn as amuletic jewelry to protect against evil influences and accidental injuries. Back in the Middle Ages, amber necklaces were hung around the necks of small children as amulets to cure or ward off croup. Amber is sacred to the goddess Freya.

Amethyst

Amethyst is a gemstone of power, peace, protection, and spirituality. It helps balance the aura, controls evil thoughts, eases tension, sharpens the intellect, and brings contentment and sincerity into the lives of those who use it. At one time, its main attribute was to prevent intoxication. Amethyst is an amulet of exceptional good luck for all persons born in the month of February or under the astrological sign of Pisces. When held in the hand or placed over the Third Eye chakra, it aids spiritual and psychic development, and can be used as a powerful meditation stone. To guard against negativity, wear an amethyst pendant set in silver on a silver chain. An amethyst ring worn on the third finger of the left hand aids hunters and offers sailors and soldiers protection against harm. When engraved with a Cupid, an amethyst ring attracts true love to the wearer.

Ankh

The ankh (also known as the *crux ansata*) is an ancient Egyptian symbol resembling a cross with a loop at the top. It symbolizes the power of life and cosmic knowledge, and is the oldest and most popular amulet/religious symbol used by the Egyptians. When worn or carried, the ankh brings good health, promotes fertility, and strengthens the psychic powers.

Aquamarine

Aquamarine, a bluish-green variety of beryl, symbolizes hope and good health, and is a lucky gemstone for all persons born in the months of March and October. An aquamarine amulet enhances meditation and spiritual awareness. It also offers protection for sailors and other travelers of the sea. To attract love, wear amuletic earrings made of aquamarine.

Armadillo

To protect yourself against sorcery, negativity, and all dark forces of evil, wear or carry in your pocket an amulet in the shape of an armadillo. Bury an armadillo skull in your yard or place one over your front door to keep ghosts and demonic entities from entering your home.

Arrow

For protection from illness and to guard against the evil eye, wear an arrow-shaped pendant on a silver chain around your neck. It is interesting to note that in ancient times it was widely believed that sleeping on arrows extracted from a human body worked as a powerful love charm.

Arrowhead

Carry an arrowhead for protection against enemies, bad luck, hexes, jealousy, evil spirits, and all negative forces. Place an arrowhead over your front door (or under the mat) to prevent burglars from breaking into your home, and keep one in your car to help guard against accidents and theft.

Bat Amulet

An amulet shaped like a bat protects the wearer against hexes, enemies, and all forms of black magick when worn for one month and then thrown into a deep body of water, such as a lake or an ocean. In the state of Mississippi, it was believed that a bat's heart could bring good luck to riverboat gamblers. A bat, imaged on heliotrope or bloodstone, gives the wearer the power to control demons. In Iran, it was believed that wearing a bat's eye as an amulet could cure insomnia; while in Bohemia, the same charm was used by practitioners of magick to gain the power of invisibility. In Macedonia, where a bat is considered to be the luckiest of all living creatures, a bat's bone is often carried as an amulet to attract good luck.

Bear Amulet

Wearing a bear-claw amulet will help a woman during childbirth and increase physical strength. An amulet in the image of a bear can also be used in Neo-Pagan rituals to help invoke the powers of the lunar-goddess Diana.

Beryl

Known as both the "Mystic Stone" and the "Seer's Stone," yellow or golden beryl increases psychic abilities when placed over the Third Eye chakra or when held in the left hand during meditative rituals. When worn as amuletic jewelry, beryl is said to banish fear, strengthen the intellect, protect against enemies, promote the love of married couples, and attract the affections of the opposite sex. Once used to make crystal balls, beryl has long been used by seers as a scrying stone and as a dowsing stone to help locate lost or hidden things. To promote friendship or to reconcile enemies, engrave the image of a frog on a piece of beryl and carry it near your heart or wear it on a gold necklace. A beryl engraved with the image of the sea-god Poseidon works as a powerful amulet of protection for sailors and fishermen.

Bloodstone

Bloodstone is a mystical gemstone possessing numerous magickal properties. Wear or carry a bloodstone amulet to stimulate prophetic powers, avert lightning, conjure storms or earthquakes, or to preserve good health. This stone is also credited with having the divine power to cure inflammatory illness, heal tumors, and stop hemorrhages. Bloodstone is an especially powerful good luck amulet for all persons born in the month of March.

Buddha Amulet

Wear a golden Buddha charm on a necklace or bracelet, or carry a small jade Buddha as an amulet to bring good luck and wealth into your life.

Bull Amulet

To increase fertility in women and virility in men, wear a bull-shaped amulet, or place one under the bed before making love. When worn as jewelry, the symbol of the bull protects the wearer against all maledictions, procures the favor of magistrates, and brings extra special good luck to persons born under the astrological sign of Taurus.

Buzzard Feathers

To cure or prevent rheumatism, according to folklore, wear a feather from a buzzard behind one of your ears. A charm bag filled with buzzard feathers is believed by some to alleviate teething pain when tied around the neck of a child. Buzzard feathers have also been used in Native American exorcisms to drive away evil spirits, and in certain Hoodoo spells to cause an enemy to be driven insane.

Carbuncle

Wear or carry a carbuncle as an amuletic gemstone to increase wealth and power, to stimulate the heart, or to ward off nightmares, melancholia, and evil or negative thoughts. The carbuncle was used in ancient Greece to protect young children against accidental drowning. In both India and Arabia, it was employed as a protective amulet by soldiers. In the Christian tradition, the carbuncle represents the sacrifice of Jesus Christ.

Carnelian

Carnelian is a legendary stone of good luck, courage, and fertility, and a powerful good luck amulet for all persons born in the month of August. In ancient Egypt (where it was known as the "Blood of Isis Stone"), people wore amulets of carnelian for protection against the wrath of the Sun God, and to counteract the power of the evil eye. Many believed that carnelian possessed the power to prevent or heal flesh wounds, cure tumors and respiratory diseases, and keep evil spirits at bay. Wear a carnelian amulet ring to preserve tranquillity in the midst of turmoil.

Cat Amulet

The cat is a beautiful and mysterious creature, the traditional familiar of Witches, and an animal deified by the ancient Egyptians. The cat and its symbol are sacred to many Pagan goddesses, including Freya (the Norse goddess of marriage, fruitfulness, and fertility) and Bast (the Egyptian cat-goddess). Folk legend and superstition claim that all cats have nine lives, and that it is unlucky for a black cat to cross your path. (However, it is also said that owning a black cat will bring peace and good luck to the home.) Farmers in the Transylvania region of central Romania use cats as living fertility charms; while in Haiti and Africa, practitioners of the Voodoo religions use the various parts of a dead cat (such as eyes, bones, heart, etc.) as powerful charms of magick. According to one book of Hoodoo magick, to promote fertility in women, wear nine cat's claws on a necklace or carry them inside a charm bag. A cat-shaped jade amulet is believed to help ease the pains of childbirth when placed over a woman's navel during delivery. Wear any type of cat-shaped jewelry as an amulet to stimulate or increase telepathic powers, improve night vision, protect against evil entities, or make secret wishes come true. Cat-shaped amulets can also be worn or carried to attract good luck, and are especially favorable for all persons born under the astrological signs of Capricorn and Pisces.

Cat's Eye

To ward off the power of the evil eye, wear or carry a cat's eye gemstone. According to folklore and medieval legend, the cat's eye possesses the supernatural power to make its wearer invisible, to ward off all forms of sorcery, protect against financial ruin, and cure all eye ailments, chronic diseases, asthma, and croup.

Caul

The caul (a membrane that sometimes clings to the head and face of a newborn baby) has been considered a good luck omen since ancient times. It is used as a natural amulet to protect sailors and sea travelers against shipwrecks and drowning, and to guard against demons, black magick, and psychic attack. According to folklore, a caul can give its possessor the power to see and communicate with the spirits of the dead. In days of old, it was not an uncommon custom for cauls to be bought and sold (usually at expensive prices).

Chalcedony

Wear or carry a blue chalcedony gemstone as an amulet to secure public favor, chase away the blues, protect against evil entities and dangers at sea, and attract good luck. To increase the supply of breast milk, nursing mothers should wear white chalcedony on a golden necklace, according to an old Italian custom. Chalcedony is sacred to the goddess Diana and should be worn or kept on the altar when performing any rituals in her honor.

Coral

Wear or carry a piece of pure red coral as a natural amulet to protect against demonic forces, all forms of black magick, and the destructive power of the evil eye. Hang a piece of coral (any color) in your home or office to keep away evil spirits and negative influences; on your bedpost to prevent unpleasant dreams, night-sweats, and visitations by succubi or incubi; in your car to guard against accidents and thieves; on fruit trees to ensure fruitfulness. To attract a new lover into your life, wear or carry a piece of pink coral as a love amulet.

Crab Amulet

An amulet in the shape of, or bearing the image of, a crab brings good luck to persons born under the astrological sign of Cancer. To increase fertility or to attract love into your life, carry or wear a pair of crab claws on a necklace.

Crescent Moon

The crescent moon is a sacred symbol of the Goddess, and also a symbol of magick, fertility, and the secret powers of Nature. Wear a piece of pink quartz shaped like a crescent moon as a love charm to attract a lover or soul mate, or as a woman's amulet to promote fertility. Moon-shaped amulets are said to be extremely lucky for all persons born under the Moon-ruled astrological sign of Cancer.

Cross

The cross is one of the oldest of mystical symbols, and in the *Encyclopedia Heraldica,* there are over 385 different varieties listed. In Christianity, the cross is an important symbol of Jesus Christ's death and resurrection. However, the symbol of the cross is actually not of Christian origin, as many believe. It was widely used by Pagan cultures in pre-Christian times as both a religious symbol and magickal tool, and did not become a symbol of the Christian tradition until about the fifth century. When worn as an amulet, the cross protects the wearer from the dark forces of evil, jinx, and bad luck. Crosses are used in many Voodoo rituals and Hoodoo spells, and they are often worn as protective amulets by spiritual healers and card readers to dispel against negative influences. For best results, a cross should be made out of gold and anointed once a day with either myrrh oil or holy water.

Crown Ring

Wear a ring shaped like a crown to bring success at work, and to attract good luck when engaging in any form of gambling. A crown ring can also be worn as a powerful love-drawing amulet.

Deer Amulet

To increase fertility, place the horns of a deer under your bed or hang them on a wall in your bedroom and rub them for a few minutes before making love with your partner.

Diamond

The diamond is a highly valued gemstone that symbolizes peace, fidelity, innocence, and serenity. It is a powerful good luck charm for all persons born under the astrological sign of Aries. When worn as amuletic jewelry, it prevents nightmares, protects sleeping women from incubi, balances both positive and negative energies, and brings confidence, divine wisdom, and consciousness. In the Middle Ages, diamonds were used as amulets against poison, plague, pestilence, and sorcery. To ward off enemies, madness, and all wild and venomous beasts, according to medieval legend, hold a diamond in your left hand as you recite the Lord's Prayer.

Dog Amulet

To keep all malicious or evil persons and spirits from gaining entrance to your home, bury five dog-shaped amulets on each side of your house.

Dolphin Amulet

For protection against accidents when traveling by ship, wear or carry an amulet shaped like or bearing the image of a dolphin.

Donkey Amulet

Carry or wear a donkey-shaped amulet when you are in need of extra special good luck. The figure of a donkey, when engraved on a chrysolite and worn around the neck on a gold chain, will increase the wearer's psychic powers of prediction.

Dove Amulet

To bring peace into your home or workplace, wear a dove-shaped amulet on a chain around your neck. The symbol of the turtle dove protects the wearer against death, fire, and lightning. The dove is a bird sacred to Ishtar, Aphrodite, and other goddesses of love and fertility.

Dragon

The mystical dragon is an ancient Chinese symbol of the male element known as yang. Wear any dragon-shaped jewelry as an amulet for love and happiness, or to promote fertility. Keep a small jade dragon in your home to dispel all negative vibrations and bad luck. The figure of a dragon, engraved on a ruby, will attract good health to its possessor, according to ancient belief.

Eagle Amulet

The eagle symbolizes swiftness and is a sacred bird of the Greek god Zeus. An eagle feather or an amulet in the shape of an eagle is said to protect people and structures against lightning.

Egyptian Amulets

Wear or carry a King Tut amulet to attract money; a Nefertiti amulet to inspire love or to keep a lover faithful; and a mummy-shaped amulet to ward off all negative forces, bad spirits, and evil influences. To bring prosperity in business, wear or carry a gold feather amulet (an ancient Egyptian symbol of wealth). For protection against evil, wear an Egyptian cartouche pendant. The gods and goddesses of the Egyptian pantheon are also powerful magickal symbols and they are quite popular among many modern Witches. Jewelry amulets in their divine images can be easily obtained at most occult shops, mail order Witchcraft supply catalogues, psychic fairs, and gift shops that specialize in New Age jewelry. The following list contains most of the popular Egyptian deity amulets, along with their usages: Wear or carry an Isis amulet to increase fertility and to enhance all forms of enchantment; an Osiris amulet to increase male virility; a Thoth amulet for wisdom and literary inspiration, and as a good-luck charm for writers and poets; a Hathor amulet for musical inspiration and to attract love, increase fertility, and protect infants; a Min amulet to increase fertility and also for protection while traveling; a Ra amulet for good luck and wealth; a Ptah amulet for stability and as a good-luck charm for architects, sculptors, and craftsmen; and a Mut amulet to increase fertility. A Bast amulet ensures good health and increases sexual passion. It can also be attached to the collar of your cat-familiar to keep him or her safe from all dangers. Put an Anubis amulet on the collar of your dog-familiar to help guard him or her against all negative forces. (For more Egyptian amulets, see *ANKH, EYE OF HORUS, PYRAMID AMULET, SCARAB BEETLE AMULET,* and *SNAKE AMULET.*)

Elk Tooth Amulet

Wear or carry in a pocket or charm bag the tooth of an elk as a powerful amulet to dispel negativity and attract good fortune into your life.

Emerald

The emerald is a symbol of peace, love, and eternal life. When worn or carried as an amulet, it strengthens love, intelligence, eloquence, and popularity; and it was once believed that emerald charms worn by pregnant women could offer them protection against miscarriages. Another ancient belief was that an emerald placed under the tongue could give a mortal man the power to prophesy. Emerald amulets increase psychic sensitivity when held over the Third Eye chakra; and when worn on a finger as a ring, this gemstone warns the wearer against poisons, strengthens the memory, protects against demonic possession, and ensures success in love. When carried by travelers, an emerald amulet brings good luck and is believed to calm storms at sea.

Evil Eye Countercharms

The evil eye (also known as "fascination," "overlooking," and "jettatura") is the inborn supernatural power to cause bewitchment, harm, misfortune or death to others by an angry or venomous glance of the eye. The evil eye is greatly feared by many people in nearly all regions of the world, and countless magickal spells, charms, talismans, and incantations have been used for protection against it. Among the numerous anti-evil eye amulets that exist, the most popular ones are the curved horn mounted in gold and worn on a chain around the neck, and the clenched hand with thumb placed between the index and middle fingers (known as the "fig"). These two amulets, which are quite popular in Italy as well as in the United States, are phallic in nature and date back to ancient times. The image of the human eye (especially the "Eye of Horus") is another well-known and effective amulet against the evil eye, and it was very popular among the ancient Egyptians. Both the Star of David symbol (also known as "Solomon's Seal") and the Hand of Fatima have also been used by many to neutralize or reverse the effects of the evil eye. Other objects used as evil eye countercharms include: garlic worn around the neck, iron keys placed between the eyes, blue-colored beads, gold crosses, crucifixes, porcelain eyes, earrings, noserings, shamrocks, seashells, fans, whistles, bells, mirrors, brass, coral, fringe, red ribbon, snake symbols, and various animal-shaped amulets.

Eye of Horus

Also known as the "Udjat" or "All-Seeing Eye," the Eye of
Horus is an ancient symbol associated with the occult
sciences and used in modern Witchcraft as an amulet for
wisdom, prosperity, spiritual protection, good health, the
increasing of clairvoyant powers, and protection against
thieves and the evil eye. In ancient Egypt, the Eye of Horus
was one of the most popular and important magickal
symbols and was used as a funerary amulet to guard against
evil forces and for rebirth in the underworld.

Fairy Amulet

Wear any type of fairy-shaped jewelry as an amulet to
increase magickal powers, enhance all enchantments and
bewitchments, attract fairy-folk, and put your spirit in
harmony with Mother Nature.

Fish Amulet

An amulet shaped like a pair of fish and made of gold or mother-of-pearl will increase fertility and virility, bring prosperity, and offer you protection from people who might hate you or have evil intentions. For persons born under the astrological sign of Pisces, the fish is an especially powerful good luck amulet.

Fluorite

Fluorite is a gemstone that increases psychic awareness and cosmic understanding when placed over the Third Eye chakra during meditative rituals.

Four-Leaf Clover

Good fortune will smile on you if you carry a four-leaf clover, or if you wear a pin, ring, or pendant shaped like one. The four-leaf clover (a highly magickal plant and a powerful amulet of Irish origin) is believed to be the most powerful of all natural amulets, and is especially favorable for persons born under the astrological signs of Cancer and Pisces. It was sacred to the Trinity, and was used by the ancient Druids as a charm against evil and to attain clairvoyant powers.

Fox Amulet

Wear or carry an amulet bearing the image of a fox for prosperity or to aid in the development of shape-shifting powers.

Frog Amulet

To promote friendship or reconcile enemies, engrave the image of a frog on a piece of beryl and carry it near your heart or wear it as a necklace. A frog amulet is also good for increasing fertility and virility.

Gambling Amulets

(See CROWN RING; INDIAN HEAD AMULET; PLAYING CARDS AMULET; SKULL AND CROSSBONES.)

Garlic

Garlic is one of the oldest and most famous of natural protection amulets used throughout the world in a variety of ways to keep away vampires, sorcerers, demonic spirits, and all forms of evil. It is also used by many Witches and Shamans as a healing amulet. Garlic is said to be ruled by Mars and under the influence of Aries and Scorpio.

Garnet

Also known as the "Passion Stone," the garnet is a balancer of the yin/yang energies. It increases psychic sensitivity and sexual energy. Garnet is an ideal gemstone to use during meditative rituals, and it can be worn as amuletic jewelry to attract sexual love and soul mates. When placed under a pillow or worn while sleeping, it wards off bad dreams and evil spirits of the night. A garnet engraved with the symbol of a lion is a powerful amulet for attracting good health and success. It also protects the wearer from all dangers when traveling. To attract a lover, wear a heart-shaped garnet amulet in a red velvet charm bag over your heart. (Be sure to anoint it every Friday night with three drops of rose or patchouli oil.)

Goat Amulet

The symbol of the goat (sacred to Aphrodite and the Horned God) increases fertility when worn or carried as an amulet, and is especially favorable as a good-luck charm for persons born under the astrological sign of Capricorn. The image of two goats engraved on an onyx is said to give a magician the power to summon and control spirits.

Hand of Glory

In medieval times, a gruesome candleholder made from the mummified hand of a hanged criminal and known as the "Hand of Glory" was employed as a magickal charm by thieves and sorcerers to achieve invisibility, open locked doors, and paralyze or put victims into a deep trancelike state. According to legend, the only way to protect oneself against the Hand of Glory and to render the charm powerless is to extinguish its candle flame with milk. Today, the Hand of Glory is merely a wax candle in the shape of a hand. It is burned for good luck and to ward off all forms of evil, especially the evil eye.

Hedgehog Amulet

In Morocco, it is believed that the destructive power of the evil eye cannot harm a child who wears the jawbone of a hedgehog on a necklace.

Hematite

Hematite was a sacred stone used by the warriors of ancient Rome and Greece as an amulet to protect against wounds, and to increase courage on the battlefield.

Horn

The gold horn is a popular necklace-charm worn by Italians as an amulet against the evil eye. When worn by a man, the horn (an ancient and obvious phallic symbol) increases sex appeal and promotes male virility. Compare *PHALLUS*.

Horseshoe

The horseshoe is a well-known good luck symbol in many parts of the world. According to superstition, nail an iron horseshoe over your door with the convex side pointing up for protection against sorcery, bad luck, and the evil eye. For good luck, nail it over your door with the convex side pointing down. Wear any type of horseshoe-shaped jewelry or carry miniature horseshoe charms in a mojo charm bag to promote fertility, guard against evil, and attract good luck. To ward off bad luck and negativity, wear a ring made of horseshoe nails.

Hyacinth

The hyacinth is a transparent red, brown, or orange variety of zircon. Wear a hyacinth gemstone on a necklace or mounted in a ring to ease the pain of childbirth. The amuletic powers of hyacinth can also be used for protection against negative supernatural forces.

Indian Head Amulet

For protection against all negative influences and evil spirits, wear an Indian-head coin on a chain around your neck or carry one in a purse, pocket, or mojo charm bag. The symbol of the Indian head is considered by many to be the most powerful of amulets, and it can be used also as a good-luck charm when gambling. To promote peace in the home, wear an amulet with the popular symbol of the Indian Chief, or hang it in your house to exercise control over your family and the things around you.

Iron Protection Amulet

To protect yourself against sorcery and all malevolent supernatural beings, wear an iron bracelet or sleep with a piece of iron under your bed. In Burma, iron pyrites are commonly used as amulets to protect the wearer against crocodile attacks, and in many parts of Europe, they are used to protect against lightning.

Jack Amulet

A "jack" is a powerful amulet used by practitioners of folk magick in the southern regions of the United States (especially Mississippi). It consists of a piece of red flannel shaped like a human finger and stuffed with coal dust and dirt, and contains a silver dime. After being charged with magickal power by an incantation invoking the presence and help of the old gods, a jack amulet can be worn or carried to prevent a traveler from losing his or her way.

Jacinth

Jacinth aids astral projection and increases psychic powers. It is often worn or carried as an amulet for the attainment of honor, prudence, and wisdom. It is also reputed to protect against poisonings, lightning, injuries and wounds. Wear a jacinth ring to dispel all evil, or place a jacinth amulet over the navel during delivery to help ease the pains of childbirth. In Italy, jacinth is used as the birthstone for persons born in the month of January.

Jade

Jade is a mystical gemstone sacred to the Chinese goddess of healing mercy. It is the symbol of tranquillity and wisdom. It is said to possess yang (the vital masculine principle), and in China, it was believed to impart immortality. When worn as amuletic jewelry, jade prevents nightmares, heals many diseases, and prolongs life. Wear a jade butterfly as an amulet to attract love and good luck. A jade statue placed in the house near a window or in the garden will avert lightning. To ease the pains of childbirth, place a small jade figure of Kuan Yin over the navel during delivery.

Jasper

Jasper is an energizing gemstone that strengthens the intellect when worn as an amulet with certain Cabalistic inscriptions. It is sacred to the goddess Isis, and is used by many to counteract the power of the evil eye, ease the pain of childbirth, and protect against wounds and hemorrhages. Green jasper repels ghosts, helps reduce fevers, and wards off bites of serpents. Black jasper is used by farmers in Italy as an amulet against lightning.

Jet

Jet is a dense velvet-black coal that takes a high polish and is used as jewelry (especially women's mourning jewelry). It is often called the "Exorcism Stone" and is ruled by the planet Saturn. Carry an amulet of jet in your pocket, purse, or charm bag to protect yourself against the evil eye and to ward off all demonic forces.

Lamb Amulet

To increase fertility or to fill your home with peace, use an amulet in the shape of a lamb (the symbol of fertility and peace). .

Lapis Lazuli

Lapis lazuli is a powerful love-drawing gemstone dedicated to the goddesses Aphrodite, Venus, and Isis. It aids meditation and psychic development when placed over the Third Eye chakra. It is frequently used by Witches in love spells and as amulets against negative influences and malevolent supernatural forces. Lapis lazuli is also a powerful good luck charm when worn by persons born under the astrological sign of Capricorn.

Leprechaun Amulet

The leprechaun is the most famous of all magickal creatures in Irish folklore. Wear any type of leprechaun-shaped jewelry as an amulet for good luck and wealth. The leprechaun amulet is especially lucky for those who are Irish.

Lightning Bolt Pendant

Wear a circular sterling silver pendant with a lightning-bolt symbol painted or engraved on it as an amulet to awaken or increase your spellcasting powers.

Lightning Protection Amulets

To protect yourself from being struck by lightning, according to an old book of Witchcraft and Wizardry, dig up a small black coal from under a mugwort plant at either noon or midnight on the Summer Solstice and carry it with you in a pocket, purse, or charm bag as a powerful protective amulet. A piece of wood splintered from a tree by a bolt of lightning or cut from a lightning-struck tree also works well as a powerful amulet against lightning when carried in your pocket. In some parts of England it was once believed that a sprig of hawthorn cut on Holy Thursday could be used as an amulet to guard a family and their home from being struck by lightning.

Lion Amulet

The lion (or "King of Beasts") symbolizes courage, boldness, and nobility. Wearing lion-shaped jewelry will help to cure shyness, overcome enemies, protect you against danger while traveling, and strengthen your emotions. Throughout the Middle Ages, images of lions were carved on special amulet stones or stamped on various metals and used to treat kidney ailments and acute intestinal pains. When engraved on a garnet, the symbol of the lion brings good health and success to the wearer; and when imaged on a jasper, it is said to cure fevers and guard against all poisons. A lion amulet brings exceptional good luck to all persons born under the astrological sign of Leo.

Lodestone

Lodestones are magnetized pieces of magnetite. They have long been used by practitioners of white magick to set up energy fields that block out negative vibrations. In olden times, amulets made from lodestones were worn to guard against snakebites, and it is said that a lodestone placed in the right ear will enable a mortal man or woman to hear the voices of Pagan deities.

Love Amulets

To awaken passion and tenderness in your beloved, wear any of the following: an amuletic necklace of seashells, a consecrated golden key or wedding ring on a chain, a locket containing the image of any Pagan love deity, a carved jade butterfly, a holed pebble on a string or gold chain, or a copper bracelet (sacred to Venus, the Roman goddess of love). The fruit of the mandrake (often called "love apples") and all roots, flowers, herbs, and fruits ruled by Venus can be used as love amulets. Carry or wear any of the following gemstone amulets to transmit your love vibrations and attract a soul mate: amethyst (only if you were born under the astrological sign of Taurus or Gemini), beryl, moonstone (only if you were born under the astrological sign of Cancer), ruby, rutilated quartz, star sapphire, or turquoise. To attract or strengthen love, wear an emerald or a lodestone (sacred to both Venus and Aphrodite) on a Friday. To reconcile a broken love affair or ensure faithfulness in a relationship, wear a diamond ring as an amulet and anoint it once a day with three drops of rose, patchouli, or lavender oil. (See also: *ARROW, CORAL, CROWN RING, MOONSTONE, PEACOCK AMULET, VENUS PENTACLE,* and *WISHBONE.*) For more information on love amulets, please read my book, *The Secrets of Love Magick* (Citadel Press, 1992).

Mandrake Root

The mandrake is a poisonous, narcotic plant associated with medieval Witchcraft and sorcery, and believed to be the most magickal of all plants and herbs. It is potent in all forms of enchantment, and is regarded as a powerful aphrodisiac by the Orientals. Mandrake is ruled by the planet Venus, and its human-shaped root is used as an amulet to increase psychic powers, promote female fertility and male virility, reveal treasures, and inspire passion and romance.

Money-Drawing Amulets

To attract riches and prosperity, wear or carry a gold cornucopia charm (also known as a "Horn of Plenty"), a garnet stone in the shape of a lion, a jade Buddha, or any type of amuletic jewelry in the shape of a ladybug, a green grasshopper, a spider, or the sun.

Moonstone

To see into the future, according to an ancient grimoire of the magickal arts, place a moonstone amulet in your mouth at night when the Moon is full. Wear a ring of moonstone (dedicated to the love-goddess Aphrodite) as amuletic jewelry to attract a soul mate, inspire tender passions, or to protect a love. Carry a moonstone in a charm bag to attract good luck or prevent nervousness. The powers of the moonstone (also known as the "Stone of Love") are extremely potent when it is worn or carried by persons born under the Moon-ruled astrological sign of Cancer.

Onyx

An onyx amulet protects its wearer from danger and misfortunes, stimulates the mind, brings courage and strength, increases spiritual wisdom, and dispels negativity. Onyx is ruled by the planet Saturn, and therefore possesses a powerful Capricorn/Aquarius vibration. In India, onyx is used as a charm to counteract the evil eye and also to control amorous desires.

Opal

A powerful amulet for persons born under the astrological sign of Libra, the opal increases clairvoyant powers, balances the psyche, sharpens the memory, attracts good fortune, and gives healing power to the wearer. Opal is ruled by the Moon, and is sacred to all lunar deities. Black opal is considered to be one of the luckiest gemstones in the world for all twelve signs of the zodiac.

Owl Amulet

To increase knowledge, wear an owl-shaped pendant made of gold, silver, or copper. The symbol of the owl (sacred to the goddess Athena) also brings good luck, especially to all persons born under an Earth sign: Taurus, Virgo, Capricorn.

Peace Amulet

To bring peace within and around you, to end conflicts, or to aid in meditation, wear any type of amuletic jewelry in the shape of a peace sign (a symbol popular among young people during the 1960s and even today.)

Peacock Amulet

To receive the power of immortality, according to an ancient grimoire of magick, wear an amulet in the shape of a peacock on a gold chain around your neck. A peacock amulet can also be used in Pagan rituals to help invoke the powers of Isis, the ancient Egyptian goddess of fertility. According to old folk-superstition, the feathers of the peacock are considered to be extremely unlucky and, if worn or brought into the house, will prevent a woman from ever marrying or giving birth to a child. According to the *Kama Sutra*, a man can make himself irresistible to the opposite sex by covering the bone of a peacock with gold and wearing it tied to his right hand as a love charm.

Pearls

Pearls are sacred to all lunar deities, and are a part of nearly every love charm of the Orient. They can be worn in the form of amuletic jewelry or carried in charm bags as amulets for healing, to protect against fire, and to ward off evil. Pearls are ruled by the Moon, and are said to be powerful lucky charms for all persons born under the astrological sign of Cancer. (Please note: Pearls must be worn constantly to keep them from losing their amuletic power.)

Pentagram

This is one of the most powerful and important Pagan symbols used by Witches and ceremonial magicians alike. The pentagram (a five-pointed star within a circle) represents the four mystical and ancient elements of Fire, Water, Air, and Earth, surmounted by the Spirit. Wearing any type of jewelry in the shape of, or bearing the symbol of, the pentagram will help open your mind to the mysteries of magick, increase psychic awareness, protect against evil spirits and all negative forces, and strengthen your spellcasting powers.

Pentalpha Amulet

Wear a silver ring engraved with a pentalpha (a magickal and powerful design formed by five interlocking A's) to help awaken or strengthen your divinatory powers or to aid in the conjuration of beneficent spirits.

Phallus

Wear any type of phallus-shaped amulet on a necklace, or carry one in a charm bag to increase male virility and sexual magnetism. Phallus amulets were commonly used in ancient times by various cultures (particularly the Greeks and Romans) to avert the evil eye.

Pheasant Amulet

Wear or carry a pheasant-shaped amulet for safety and protection when traveling by airplane.

Playing Cards Amulet

Wear a gold charm in the image of playing cards on a chain around your neck as an amulet to bring success and to attract riches when gambling or playing cards. (To make the playing-cards amulet even luckier, engrave or paint your name, birthdate, and lucky numbers on the back and anoint it daily with three drops of honeysuckle, myrrh, or spearmint oil.)

Pyramid Amulet

Wear a pyramid amulet to improve work habits, increase or re-energize your psychic powers, or to attract good luck into your life. Crystals shaped like pyramids possess the power to balance emotional qualities and are said to bring wisdom. When placed under a bed, they protect the sleeper from all forms of psychic attack, unpleasant dreams, succubi, incubi, and other evil spirits of the night. The power of the pyramid is also believed by many to enhance meditations and past-life regressions, speed the healing of wounds and burns, cure headaches and insomnia, break unhealthy addictions, and even revive ailing houseplants.

Quartz Crystals

Also known as "Rain-Stones," quartz crystals are commonly used in the rainmaking ceremonies of many Aboriginal tribes in Australia. Quartz crystals are used as divining stones by the Cherokee Indians; and in certain parts of Europe and the Middle East, they are used as amulets to increase breast milk in nursing mothers, and to cure sterility.

Rabbit's Foot

The rabbit's foot is perhaps the most popular amulet used in modern times. It is usually carried on a keychain or worn on a necklace to ward off accidents and evil, and to increase good luck, happiness, and fertility.

Ram Amulet

An amulet in the shape of a ram will increase fertility in women. It also brings exceptional good luck to persons born under the astrological sign of Aries.

Ruby

As a powerful amulet, the ruby works best for those born under the astrological sign of Leo. It brings peace of mind, stimulates sexuality, removes all evil and impure thoughts, protects against tempests, banishes sorrow, and prevents nightmares. A heart-shaped ruby amulet attracts love when worn over the heart or carried in a red velvet charm bag filled with seashells and Venus-ruled herbs.

Saint Christopher Medallion

This is a powerful amulet of protection. Wear it on a necklace or carry it in a purple flannel charm bag for protection against accidents and misfortune while traveling. (Saint Christopher is the patron saint of travelers.)

Sapphire

Sapphire is a gemstone with many supernatural powers, and it is the symbol of harmony and peace. When worn as an amulet, the sapphire brings happiness and contentment, and protects the wearer against misfortune, fraud, the wrath of enemies, violence, the evil eye, sorcery, psychic attack, and accidental death. Place a sapphire over your Third Eye chakra to stimulate psychic energies or to see into the future. The sapphire brings exceptional good luck to persons born under the astrological sign of Taurus and all who are born in the month of April.

Sardonyx

When worn or carried as an amulet, the sardonyx stone prevents miscarriages and guards against sorcery. To all persons born under the astrological sign of Leo, it brings love, happiness, good luck, and prosperity.

Scarab Beetle Amulet

One of the most famous of all Egyptian amulets, the sacred scarab is an emblem of the Great Creator of the Universe. It is a symbol of perpetual renewal of life, and is sacred to the god Khepera. Wear scarab beetle jewelry for good luck and protection against all evil forces.

Scorpion Amulet

If you were born under the astrological sign of Scorpio, carry or wear a scorpion-shaped amulet to attract good luck, repel all evil and negative forces, and guard against enemies.

Seal of Solomon

Also known as the "Star of David," the Seal of Solomon dates back to the Bronze Age and is a powerful symbol with many mystical and magickal qualities. Before becoming the most prominent symbol of Judaism, the six-pointed star was used by alchemists and ceremonial magicians in the preparation of amulets. It was also a part of early Celtic magick and was employed by Druid priests as a magick seal against evil ghosts. of the night. As an amulet, the Seal of Solomon is believed to offer protection against both enemies and the evil eye, control spirits, and bring good luck in all aspects of life. In parts of West Africa, the Seal of Solomon is the symbol of ardent love.

Shark Amulet

The shark symbolizes great strength, and an amulet bearing its image is believed to exert powerful control over any person who comes within its magickal aura. In Hawaii and other parts of the world, it is believed by some that wearing shark's teeth on a necklace will bring good fortune, keep away evil spirits, and protect surfers against accidents and shark attacks.

Skeleton Key Amulet

Wear an old skeleton key on a chain around your neck as an amulet to open the doors of opportunity and success, guard against the evil eye, and repel sorcery and all evil spirits.

Skull Amulet and Spell

To help break the chains of any addiction, wear a gold skull-shaped charm on a necklace as a magickal amulet. Rub the skull three times a day while focusing your eyes upon it and thinking about the misery that your addiction brings. After three months, remove the skull from the chain and throw the amulet into a moving body of water.

Skull and Crossbones

A symbol of death once used by pirates and more recently as a warning label on poisons, the skull and crossbones can be used as a powerful amulet to protect the wearer against Voodoo, Hoodoo, and Santeria black magick. It possesses the power to reverse any hex and return the evil to the person who cast it upon you. This symbol is also popular among gamblers, as it is believed to keep their good luck from turning bad.

Snake Amulet

Wear a rattlesnake's rattle on a necklace as a powerful amulet to increase wisdom and sexual powers. In ancient Egypt, red stones carved into the shape of a serpent's head were believed to possess the supernatural power to prevent venomous snakes from biting. Snake symbols were commonly used on ancient Gypsy charms to protect the wearer from the powers of the dreaded evil eye.

Staurolite

Cross-shaped staurolite crystals (also known as "Fairy Stones") can be worn or carried as amulets to protect against all forms of evil magick and to attract good luck. Fill a green velvet charm bag with staurolite and white rowan tree blossoms and wear it on a string around your neck to attract benevolent fairy-folk.

Sun Symbol

Carry a gold charm shaped like the Sun in a gold or yellow-colored velvet charm bag if you wish to acquire wealth, good health, success and/or fame. This is also an effective amulet to use if you feel that others have been causing you trouble. The symbol of the Sun is sacred to all solar deities, and is especially powerful for all persons born under the astrological sign of Leo.

Swallow Amulet

To attract good luck into your life, wear a swallow-shaped amulet made of sterling silver. To keep your home safe from evil sorcery, ghosts, fire, and lightning, attach a purple charm bag filled with swallow feathers to your chimney or roof.

Thunderbird Symbol

Used by Native Americans of the Northwest United States as a weatherworking symbol to attract rain, thunder, and lightning, the thunderbird is a powerful protection amulet and is reputed to bring good luck to gamblers.

Tiger Amulet

According to ancient Chinese folklore, to attain physical strength, immortality, or the ability to master the super-natural art of shapeshifting, wear a consecrated silver or jade amulet bearing the image of a tiger.

Tiki

Use a tiki amulet to restore or preserve male sexual potency. The tiki is of Polynesian origin and represents the first man on Earth created from red clay by the god Tane (one of the chief deities of many Polynesian mythologies). The tiki should be carved from nephrite or whalebone and worn on a chain around the neck.

Topaz

Topaz is an energizing gemstone that stimulates the intellect, increases courage, and dispels negativity. Wear any type of topaz jewelry as an amulet to protect against injury or attack. A topaz bracelet worn on the left wrist will keep away evil spirits and all forms of enchantment. Topaz is said to bring happiness, longevity, beauty, intelligence, and good luck when worn by persons born in November.

Tourmaline

Tourmaline is a gemstone that symbolizes vitality. Carry one in a mojo bag as an amulet to protect against illness, or wear a tourmaline as amuletic jewelry to attract a lover into your life. Black tourmaline deflects negativity, dispels fears, and balances the aura. It connects the physical with the spiritual, and reduces anger, jealousy, and feelings of insecurity. Green tourmaline, also known as "verdelite," possesses the power to attract money and success. Pink tourmaline, also known as "rubellite," calms, reduces fear, protects the aura against negativity, and induces peaceful sleep. Watermelon tourmaline heals the emotions, balances sexual energies, and stabilizes the yin/yang polarities. Yellow tourmaline stimulates the brain, strengthens the psychic powers, and increases both wisdom and understanding.

Tulip Bulb Amulet

Carry a tulip bulb as a natural amulet to bring love into your life. Wear a tulip bulb on a string around your neck or sleep with one under your pillow at night to attract a new lover, increase sex appeal, or induce romantic dreams. Wear or carry an amulet shaped like a tulip to promote fertility in females and virility in males.

Turquoise

Turquoise is a mystical gemstone sacred to the Native Americans of the Southwest United States. In the Orient, it is used as a protective charm for horses and their riders. In Mexico, it is a popular amulet for attracting good luck. To protect against evil influences, carry a piece of turquoise in a blue charm bag on a Wednesday. A carved piece of turquoise brings good fortune into a house and is said to possess the power to hypnotize wild animals. Turquoise is often worn as an evil-eye countercharm, carried or worn as an amulet to protect against venomous bites, poison, blindness, assassinations, and accidental deaths. Turquoise absorbs negative feelings and possesses a strong healing vibration.

Turtle Amulet

For spiritual protection, compassion, stimulation of creativity, and strengthening of divinatory powers, wear a gold turtle-shaped charm on a chain around your neck as an amulet or carry one in a white mojo charm bag. To promote female fertility, keep a tortoise shell under your bed and rub a bit of mugwort tea or musk oil on the outside of it just before engaging in lovemaking.

Unicorn Amulet

The unicorn is an ancient symbol of chastity and protection, and its fabled horn was said to be used in medieval times as an amulet to detect poisons in the food or drinks of kings, queens, pontiffs, and popes. To promote fertility or increase sexual magnetism, wear any type of amuletic jewelry shaped like a unicorn. The symbol of this magnificent mystical creature also pierces the plans of enemies and keeps the wearer safe from all evil forces.

Venus Pentacle

Wear a consecrated Venus Pentacle on a silver chain or a braided necklace of green and red threads as a magickal amulet to bring passion and romance into your life. The Venus Pentacle (which can easily be obtained at most occult supply shops and mail-order catalogues) also works well for those who desire a loving marriage mate.

Wishbone

Wear gold wishbone-shaped jewelry (or even an actual turkey or chicken wishbone on a necklace) as an amulet to attract good luck and to make wishes and dreams come true. To bring a new lover into your life, nail a wishbone over the front door of your home on New Year's Day, and thrice say: "Lover, come hither!"

Wizard Amulet

Wear any type of wizard-shaped jewelry as an amulet for wisdom, strength, and good luck, to help develop divinatory abilities, and to increase both magickal and psychic powers.

Zodiac Good Luck Gemstones

Each astrological sign of the zodiac rules one or more gemstone, known as a "birth-charm." These gemstones are used in mojo charm bags or worn as amuletic jewelry to attract good luck and to protect against evil, misfortune, and illness; however, it is considered unlucky to wear a birth-charm belonging to an astrological sign other than your own. The twelve signs of the zodiac and their corresponding good luck gemstones are as follows: *Aries*: coral and diamond; *Taurus*: carnelian and emerald; *Gemini*: agate and alexandrite; *Cancer:* moonstone, pearl, and all white-colored gemstones; *Leo*: amber, ruby, and all yellow or golden-colored gemstones; *Virgo:* sapphire and sardonyx; *Libra*: opal and tourmaline; *Scorpio*: topaz; *Sagittarius*: turquoise and zircon; *Capricorn*: garnet, lapis lazuli, and all black gemstones; *Aquarius*: amethyst and jacinth; *Pisces*: aquamarine and bloodstone.

3

Mojo Magick

A mojo is a small charm bag used to attract or dispel certain influences. It is usually made of leather or flannel, and filled with a variety of magickal items such as herbs, stones, feathers, and bones. Mojo bags can either be worn on a belt or necklace, or carried in a pocket or a purse. They are commonly used by shamans, Wiccans of the eclectic tradition, and practitioners of hoodoo. (Hoodoo is a Voodoo-like type of folk magick which is quite popular in many of the rural regions of the southern United States, particularly in Louisiana.)

For a mojo to work properly, everything put into the bag must possess the appropriate magickal vibration corresponding to the spell. For instance, a mojo bag made for the purpose of attracting a lover should contain only herbs, gemstones, or other objects associated with love magick or symbolic of romance.

To personalize and empower a mojo even more, some personal item (such as a lock of hair or fingernail clippings) from the person for whom the mojo is made should be enclosed in the bag along with the other magickal items. An appropriate birthstone or something with the person's birth-date or astrological symbol written on it also works well.

Mojo bags can be purchased at most occult shops or through many of the mail-order magickal supplies cata-logues listed in the Pagan Resources chapter, but if you prefer to make your own (which many Witches do), here are some easy instructions for you to follow:

Cut a chamois or piece of flannel (of the appropriate magickal color) into two equal-sized squares, about 3″ × 3″. Place the two squares together and sew shut three of the sides to form an open pouch. Turn it inside out and fill it with whatever magickal ingredients the spell calls for. Close the open end by folding it down about ¼-inch, like the flap of an envelope, and then either sew it shut or run a cord or thin leather strap through it as a drawstring to close the bag. (*Important note*: Before making your mojo bag be sure that you are working during the proper phase of the Moon. For more information, see *Lunar Magick* in chapter One.) After the mojo has been filled and sealed, it should be ritually cleansed of any and all negative vibra-tions immediately, and then charged with magickal power.

Mojo Consecration and Charging Ritual

Cast a clockwise circle at least six feet in diameter and erect a north-facing altar in the center of it.

At the right side of the altar (east), place a fireproof incense burner filled with frankincense and myrrh to represent the element of Air.

At the front of the altar facing you (south), place a candle of the appropriate magickal color to represent the element of Fire.

At the left side of the altar (west), place a goblet of water (either holy water from a church, or rainwater that has been blessed by a Wiccan priestess or priest) to represent the element of Water. (In place of the water, you can also use white wine, your favorite perfume or cologne, or a bottle of magickally appropriate herbal oil.)

At the rear of the altar (north), place a small cauldron or dish containing sand, soil, or salt to represent the element of Earth.

Light the candle and incense. Take the mojo bag in your right hand and pass it through the rising smoke of the incense as you say:

BY THE FOUR ANCIENT ELEMENTS
I DO CONSECRATE THIS MOJO BAG
AND DEDICATE IT AS A TOOL
OF POSITIVE WICCAN MAGICK.
O ANCIENT GODS OF AIR, AND ALL
ELEMENTAL SPIRITS OF THE EAST,
LET THIS MOJO BAG BE NOW CHARGED
WITH THE MYSTICAL ENERGY
OF YOUR DIVINE WHITE LIGHT.

Move the mojo bag three times in a clockwise circle around the flame of the candle, and say:

O ANCIENT GODS OF FIRE, AND ALL
ELEMENTAL SPIRITS OF THE SOUTH,
LET THIS MOJO BAG BE NOW CHARGED
WITH THE MYSTICAL ENERGY
OF YOUR DIVINE WHITE LIGHT.

Place the mojo bag down on the altar and proceed to anoint it with three drops of water from the goblet. With your arms outstretched, place both of your hands, palm side down, in the air about six inches above the mojo bag, and say:

O ANCIENT GODS OF WATER, AND ALL
ELEMENTAL SPIRITS OF THE WEST,
LET THIS MOJO BAG BE NOW CHARGED
WITH THE MYSTICAL ENERGY
OF YOUR DIVINE WHITE LIGHT.

The final step is to place the mojo bag in the dish or cauldron of sand, soil, or salt, and then say:

O ANCIENT GODS OF EARTH, AND ALL
ELEMENTAL SPIRITS OF THE NORTH,
LET THIS MOJO BAG BE NOW CHARGED
WITH THE MYSTICAL ENERGY
OF YOUR DIVINE WHITE LIGHT.
BLESSED BE IN THE NAME OF THE GODDESS
AND IN THE NAME OF HER CONSORT
THE GREAT HORNED GOD.
SO MOTE IT BE!

After the consecration ritual has been performed, cup the mojo bag between your hands and gently breathe upon it as you direct your thoughts and intentions into it. The charged mojo will respond to the energy of your will.

It is also a good idea never to allow anyone other than yourself (or members of your coven) to touch your mojo bag or look inside of it, as this will disturb the magickal energies and psychic vibrations that you have charged it with. (If this should ever happen, wash the mojo bag with holy water or blessed rainwater as soon as possible and then reconsecrate it by the light of a new candle of the appropriate magickal color.

To Reverse or Break the Magick of a Mojo Bag

When the Moon is in a waning phase, cast a circle at least six feet in diameter and then erect a north-facing altar within its boundary.

Upon the altar place a small cast-iron cauldron or metal ashtray, a goblet of brandy, and a goblet of holy water from a church or rainwater blessed by a Wiccan priestess or priest.

Hold the mojo bag between your hands with palms pressed gently together as if in prayer. Stand in the center of the circle. Face the east and recite the following incantation:

> AIR TURNS, FIRE BURNS,
> WATER CARRIES, EARTH BURIES.
> AS THIS MAGICK SPELL IS SPOKEN
> MAY YOUR POWER NOW BE BROKEN.

Turn yourself completely around three times in a counterclockwise direction as you will the mojo bag to lose its magickal power.

Place it in the cauldron or ashtray. Sprinkle it with a bit of the brandy and then light it with a match. As it burns, repeat the rhyming incantation.

Mix the ashes with three drops of the water and repeat the rhyming incantation.

The final step is to bury the ashes in a small hole in the ground somewhere in a quiet, undisturbed place such as a forest, a graveyard, or a secluded garden. As you fill the hole with the dug soil, repeat the magickal rhyme one last time and add the words "SO MOTE IT BE" to the end of the incantation.

Love Mojo

To attract love, fill a red or pink flannel or chamois mojo bag with some Venus-ruled herbs (such as catnip, mugwort, or yarrow), a heart-shaped piece of sun-dried lemon peel, a piece of red or pink coral, a lock of your own hair (or a clipping of your pubic hair if it is sexual love that you desire), and any of the following roots of love magick: Adam and Eve root, Beth root, ginseng root, John the Conqueror root, mandrake root, orris root.

Seal the bag; consecrate and charge it; and then wear it daily on a white string or gold chain around your neck.

If you have a particular lover in mind that you wish to attract, fix your thoughts upon that person (especially as you make the mojo bag), chant his or her name often, and secretly rub the mojo bag whenever you are in his or her presence.

To keep the magick of the love mojo potent and to prevent any negative influences and vibrations from hindering its powers, you should anoint the bag once a week on a Friday evening with three drops of pink champagne or rose oil, and then pass it through the rising smoke of burning patchouli incense.

Gambler's Lucky Mojo

When the Moon is in a waxing phase, take a nutmeg of India and drill a hole in it. Fill it with quicksilver (pure mercury), and then plug the hole with sealing wax.

Place the nutmeg of India in a red flannel mojo bag along with a High John the Conqueror root (or a Lucky Hand root), some five-fingers grass, and a highly magnetic lodestone.

Sew the bag shut so that none of the contents can fall out and then consecrate and charge it.

Once a week on a Thursday evening, anoint the outside of the mojo bag with three drops of lavender oil (or any other money-drawing oil).

Do not allow any person other than yourself to ever touch your mojo, and always carry it with you (in your pocket or purse) whenever gambling.

To keep the magick of the gambler's mojo potent, rub it daily with a silver coin (preferably one bearing the year of your birth).

Uncrossing/Hex-Breaking Mojo

To break the power of any hex or evil curse, fill a red flannel mojo bag with equal parts ague weed, dog rose, and five-finger grass.

Seal the bag; consecrate and charge it; and then carry it or wear it daily. (*IMPORTANT NOTE*: Be sure to make the mojo bag on a night when the Moon is in a waning phase, as this is the proper time to perform all forms of magick that break curses, hexes, and jinxes.)

Mojo for Getting a Job

To help your chances of getting hired on a job, fill a green flannel mojo bag with some gravel root on a night when the Moon is waxing and/or in the astrological sign of Virgo or Capricorn.

Seal the bag; consecrate and charge it; and then wear it on a belt or necklace, or carry it in your pocket or purse every time you fill out an employment application or go for a job interview.

Mojo for Protection Against Evil and Misfortune

When the Moon is full, fill a black flannel or chamois mojo bag with a handful of basil and three cloves of garlic.

Write your full name and birthdate upon a triangular piece of white wax. Anoint it with a drop of blood from your pin-pricked right thumb, and then place it inside the mojo bag.

Seal the bag; consecrate and charge it; and then wear it or carry it with you at all times. Whenever you sense the presence of evil or feel that you are in danger, rub the mojo bag and recite the following magickal incantation:

> FOR THINE PROTECTION I NOW PRAY
> LET ALL EVIL TURN AWAY
> PROTECT ME NIGHT
> PROTECT ME DAY
> AND KEEP MISFORTUNE WELL AT BAY.

Mojo to Gain Power Over Others

When the waxing Moon is in the astrological sign of Aries, Leo, or Scorpio, fill a purple flannel mojo bag with dried iron weed and a small metal or wooden pentagram upon which your full name and birthdate has been inscribed.

Seal the bag; consecrate and charge it; and then wear it or carry it with you wherever you go.

Friendship Mojo

When the Moon is in a waxing phase and/or in the astrological sign of Aquarius, fill a pink flannel mojo bag with some joe-pye weed flowers and a tulip bulb or piece of dried mandrake root upon which you have inscribed your full name, birthdate, and the sacred Pagan symbol of the five-pointed star within a circle.

Seal the bag; consecrate and charge it; and then wear or carry it in your pocket or purse to increase your popularity and win friends.

Mojo to Promote Peace, Prosperity, and Happiness

When the Moon is in a waxing phase, fill a buckskin or flannel mojo bag (either blue or white) with cattail pollen, powdered spruce needles, a piece of petrified wood, and a dove's feather.

Seal the bag; consecrate and charge it; and then wear it close to your heart.

Mojo to Induce Prophetic Dreams

When the Moon is full and/or in the astrological sign of Pisces, fill a blue flannel mojo bag with dried mugwort herb.

Seal the bag; consecrate and charge it; and keep it under your pillow at night when you sleep in order to conjure forth dreams of a prophetic nature.

Mojo to Regain Lost Manhood

When the Moon is in a waxing phase, and by the light of a burning phallus-shaped candle, fill a large buckskin or red flannel mojo bag with a mandrake root or a snake root, a horseshoe nail, a clipping of the man's pubic hair, a magnetic lodestone, a rattlesnake's rattle, a tulip bulb upon which the man's full name and birthdate have been inscribed, and a tiki amulet and/or charm shaped like a bull or fish.

Sew the bag shut. Consecrate and charge it; and then wear or carry it at all times. Rub the mojo bag on your private parts daily and prior to each time you engage in lovemaking to make you more virile.

Female Fertility Mojo

When the Moon is full, fill a green silk or flannel mojo bag with a dried mandrake root, a clipping of the woman's pubic hair, an Egyptian ankh or a dragon-shaped charm, a pair of crab claws, and any green-colored gemstone upon which the woman's full name and birthdate have been inscribed.

Seal the bag; consecrate and charge it; and then wear or carry it at all times. Rub the bag on your private parts daily and prior to each time you engage in lovemaking to make you more fertile.

Mojo to Win Court Cases

Burn dried galangal roots every night at midnight for two weeks in a row before your court date.

On the night before going to court, put the ashes in a green flannel mojo bag along with a shark's tooth and a piece of turquoise upon which your full name and birthdate and the sacred Pagan symbol of the pentagram have been inscribed.

Seal the bag; consecrate and charge it; and then wear or carry it to the courtroom to gain a favorable jury decision.

Mojo to Strengthen Psychic Powers

When the Moon is full or waxing and in the astrological sign of Aquarius or Pisces, fill a purple silk or flannel mojo bag with cloves and an Egyptian ankh.

With a flame-sterilized pin or needle, carefully prick your left thumb if you are right-handed (or right thumb if you are left-handed) and with three drops of your blood, anoint a piece of beryl gemstone upon which the symbol of the pentagram or pentalpha has been engraved. Put the beryl into the mojo bag and seal it.

After consecrating and charging it by the light of a purple candle, rub the mojo bag over your Third Eye chakra daily and during all meditative rituals, and sleep with it under your pillow every night.

Within a short period of time, you should begin to notice a marked improvement in your powers of telepathy, clairvoyance, and divination.

Passion Mojo

To put more passion into your love life or to increase your sex appeal, light a red candle (preferably apple, cinnamon, or strawberry scented) when the Moon is in a waxing phase, and fill a red flannel or silk mojo bag with a mandrake root, some dried rosebuds and petals, an Egyptian Bast amulet, and a heart-shaped piece of garnet gemstone upon which your full name (or Witch's eke-name) and birthdate have been inscribed.

Seal the mojo bag; consecrate and charge it; and wear or carry it in your pocket or purse to help make you more appealing to the opposite sex. Anoint the bag with a bit of musk oil and place it under your bed prior to lovemaking in order to increase the sexual energies of both you and your partner.

Rune Mojos

FOR PROTECTION AGAINST MISFORTUNE AND THE EVIL EYE: Wear or carry a consecrated and blessed mojo bag made of purple or black silk and filled with a handful of basil, three cloves of garlic, a rattlesnake root, a garnet or lapis lazuli gemstone, and the sacred rune stone: EOLH.

TO INCREASE YOUR HEALING POWERS: Wear or carry a consecrated and blessed mojo bag made of royal blue silk and filled with eucalyptus herb, a piece of turquoise, and the sacred healing rune stone: BOERC.

TO ATTRACT LOVE INTO YOUR LIFE: Wear or carry a consecrated and blessed mojo bag made of pink silk and filled with catnip, thyme, an Adam and Eve root, a piece of pink tourmaline or rose quartz, and the sacred rune stone: LAGU.

TO ATTRACT MONEY AND SUCCESS: Wear or carry a consecrated and blessed mojo bag made of green silk and filled with comfrey, a bayberry root, a tiger's-eye stone, a coin bearing the year of your birth, and the sacred rune stone: FEOH.

FOR PEACE AND HARMONY: Wear or carry a consecrated and blessed mojo bag made of light blue silk and filled with dried lavender, an aquamarine gemstone, a silver or gold peace-sign amulet, and the scared rune stone: MANU.

FOR WISDOM AND MIND-STRENGTHENING: Wear or carry a mojo bag made of turquoise-blue silk, blessed in the name of the goddess Minerva or Athena, and filled with sage, a piece of coral or jade, a rattlesnake's rattle, and the sacred rune stone: SIGHEL.

FOR COURAGE: Wear or carry a consecrated and blessed mojo bag made of yellow or gold silk and filled (when the Moon is in the astrological sign of Leo) with mullein, a piece of amethyst, and the sacred rune stone: TYR.

4

The Mystical Arts of Divination

Divination is, quite simply, the occult art of looking into the future or into the unknown.

It is practiced, in one form or another, by most Wiccans today, and has always been a vital part of the Witch's craft.

Before performing any type of magick, it is always wise to do a divination of some kind in order to find out whether the results of your magick will be positive or negative. This can be done by using a crystal ball, a deck of Tarot cards, candles, rune stones, or whatever method you personally prefer to use. (This is an ideal way to prevent any unintentional violations of the Wiccan Rede from occurring.)

In addition to performing divination for magickal purposes, the art is a Samhain Sabbat tradition among most Wiccans who cast rune stones or gaze into crystal balls on this mystical, most magickal night of the year.

Divination is divided into two broad categories: the reading and interpretation of omens; and any form of communication between man and spiritual entities or divine beings.

It is a fascinating art of the greatest antiquity, and its practice (both past and present) is universal.

Throughout the ages, countless methods of divination have been devised by Witches, Gypsies, shamans, Pagan priests and priestesses, medicine men, and biblical prophets.

It would be impossible to elaborate on each and every one of them in just one chapter; therefore, I have included the ones that I feel are the most popular and interesting methods of divination practiced by Wiccans and modern-day Witches alike: tassoegraphy (tea leaf reading), stolisomancy, egg divination, book divination, ceromancy, geomancy, sortition, hydatoscopy, crystal scrying, love divination, oneiromancy (divination by the interpretation of dreams), and Ouija.

Tarot card divination (or "tarotology") is perhaps the number one method of divination among most Neo-Pagans; however, I have chosen to leave it out of this chapter for the following reason:

In the average Tarot deck there are fifty-six Minor Arcana cards and twenty-two Major Arcana cards, and each one possesses its own "upright" and "reversed" divinatory meanings. In addition, each position in a Tarot spread and each of the four suits of the Minor Arcana (Wands, Swords, Cups, Pentacles) holds a unique meaning. Plus, there are numerous methods of reading the cards.

It is a complex system of divination which cannot (and should not) be condensed into a few pages or even into an entire chapter.

Therefore, I feel that a person who is interested in learning all there is to know about the art of tarotology would benefit far more by studying several complete books on the subject. (One book that I have personally read and highly recommend, especially for Tarot beginners, is *Understanding Tarot* by Jocelyn Almond and Keith Seddon, Aquarian Press, 1991.)

Tasseography

Tasseography is the art and practice of divination by interpretation of the symbolic patterns made by tea leaves in a cup.

Although generally associated with Gypsy fortunetellers, the practice of reading tea leaves dates back thousands of years to China where it was developed into a mystical science.

With a little imagination and a bit of practice, you can divine with tea leaves for yourself or for others. For best results, use China tea or an excellent grade of tea containing a minimum of tea dust. And be sure always to use a non-decorated teacup, preferably white.

For each cup to be read, put a teaspoon and a half of loose tea (not teabags) in a teapot. Add boiling water, stir vigorously, and allow it to stand for three minutes before filling your cup. The person whose fortune is being told must drink the entire cup of tea until there is just enough liquid remaining to barely cover the leaves.

If you are right-handed, pick up the cup by the handle with your left hand. If you are left-handed, pick it up with your right hand. (The reason for this is because the left side is believed to be the psychic side if you are a right-handed person, and vice versa.) Gently move the cup in a clockwise circular motion. Do this seven continuous times and then place it back in its saucer.

Gaze into the bottom of the cup. Relax and concentrate on the patterns produced by the wet tea leaves until you determine what symbolic shape the leaves have formed. And always be on the lookout for significant numbers, initials, and/or astrological symbols that might appear in or around the main pattern, as they often play an important role in the interpretation of the tea leaves.

WHAT THE SYMBOLS MEAN

AIRPLANE: Travel is in the near future for you; however, it would be wise to cancel your travel plans should the pattern be broken, for this indicates a serious accident.

ANCHOR: A safe journey or successful new project or career move is portended.

ANGEL: You will soon receive some very good news.

ANTS: There will be many difficulties to overcome before you finally reach your goal.

APPLE: A very good omen. You will achieve whatever it is you are striving for.

ARROW: You will receive an upsetting letter or telegram. Money will be involved if dots or dashes appear near the main symbol.

AXE: Beware of impending danger.

BANANA: An omen of good luck.

BASKET: You will be the recipient of a pleasant surprise. If dots and dashes are also present, a legacy of money is indicated.

BAT: This symbol indicates that your life may soon become complicated by an enemy or a higher authority. If dots and dashes are nearby, it almost always means that money matters are involved.

BEAR: A symbol of misfortune. If squares are near or touching, there is a good chance that the misfortune can be averted.

BED: This symbolizes a desire to "put to rest" problems. It can also mean that you are working too hard and are in need of some rest and relaxation.

BELL: There will be a wedding in the near future for someone who is close to you. Look for significant initials, numbers, and/or astrological symbols.

BIRD: A symbol of good luck, money, or a journey that lies ahead for you. If its wings are spread, it indicates travel by air. If leaves are close by or touching, it means you will be traveling with friends.

BOAT: This symbolizes that you possess a strong or irresistible impulse to travel.

BOTTLE: An indication that there will be an illness in the very near future. Be sure to watch your health and take extra special care in all that you do.

BOUQUET: Blissful matrimony is portended. If a number is nearby, it could signify the number of children you will have or the years the marriage will last.

BRANCH: You will form a good friendship with a person you have either met recently or will encounter in the near future.

BRIDGE: An obstacle will be overcome.

BROOM: There are new prospects ahead for you.

BULL: It is best to avoid an argument. The symbol of the bull may also represent a person born under the astrological sign of Taurus.

BUTTERFLY: A symbol of happiness, love, and beauty.

CAR: Be prepared to experience sudden changes in your surroundings. A possible move in the near future is foretold.

CASTLE: You will come into an inheritance.

CAT: A good friend or acquaintance will prove to be untrustworthy. Be mindful in whom you confide.

CHAIN: You will be receiving news of a marriage.

CIRCLE: A favorable symbol that always foretells success, whether in love, career, or health matters. If dots and dashes are close by or touching the circle, however, the success could be limited or short-lived.

CLOUDS: Beware of trouble brewing.

CLOVER: Happiness and good fortune are coming your way.

COFFIN: Be prepared to receive some disturbing news. The coffin is an ominous symbol, often indicating the death of a friend or relative.

CRESCENT MOON: For a man—think twice before taking action. It is important that you avoid rushing into hasty decisions. For a woman—a female problem is indicated.

CROSS: This is a sign that misfortune will come into your life. A sacrifice of some sort may be necessary, but in the end it will prove to be beneficial. If the cross appears inside a square, the misfortune can be averted.

CROWN: A powerful or influential friend will help you to achieve success, especially at your place of work. The symbol of the crown also signifies highest honors and praise.

CUP: You will form a long-lasting friendship with someone you have either met recently or will encounter in the very near future.

DAGGER: You will be faced with a dangerous situation. The symbol of the dagger also indicates a loss of some kind.

DOG: This symbol indicates that a friend is in need of your help. If clouds are nearby or touching, beware of unsuspected enemies.

DOOR: Be prepared for something out of the ordinary to take place.

DRAGON: A new project or career move lies ahead.

EYEGLASSES: Be prepared for a surprise in the near future. Be especially careful in all business matters.

FAN: This is an indication of a secret admirer. Be careful not to get involved in a secret love affair or you will be faced with unhappiness and embarrassment in the end.

FISH: Your future will be filled with happiness and good health. If a pair of fish appear, it may represent a person born under the astrological sign of Pisces.

FLAG: You will be forced into an unpleasant situation in which you will have to defend yourself. Be prepared to fight for what you believe is right.

FLOWER: This is a very good symbol, indicating love and happiness, and fondest wishes fulfilled. For a single, divorced, or widowed person, the possibility of a new relationship is indicated.

FOX: A trusted friend or business acquaintance will attempt to deceive you in some way.

FROG: A drastic change will take place in your life in the very near future. Be prepared for a possible change in residence or career.

GATE: You will find a solution to a problem.

GUN: It is best for you to avoid arguments with friends or family members. For men and women in the military, the symbol of the gun is an indication of active service.

HAMMER: Your hard work will pay off shortly.

HAND: An understanding friend or business acquaintance will offer you help.

HARP: Your future will be filled with romance and joy.

HAT: A happy marriage is portended if the symbol of the hat appears on the bottom of the teacup. If it appears at the side, it means honor and praise are ahead for you and your family.

HEART: A broken friendship or love affair will be restored. The symbol of the heart can also mean that an existing romance will grow stronger.

HORSESHOE: This is an obvious symbol of good luck, especially for gamblers who frequent the racetrack. Look for significant initials and/or numbers if you place bets on the horses.

HOURGLASS: It is wise to take your time before rushing into a decision. There is possible danger ahead, so think twice about a new plan or intended project.

KEY: New interests or a new opportunity is on the horizon for you. If two keys are shown, it is a warning that you could be robbed or taken advantage of.

LADDER: This is a symbol of advancement. Your ambitions will take you to high places.

LEAF or *LEAVES:* This is a symbol of renewed hope.

LINES: Straight lines indicate journeys. Indecision and frustration are portended if the lines appear wavy.

NUMBERS: Although numbers usually indicate time and are relative to other symbols in the teacup, when they appear by themselves they take on the following meanings: (1) The beginning of a new project or the birth of a child. (2) Home renovation or a change of residence in the near future. The number two also indicates a relationship. (3) The number of magick, divinity, and fate; regarded as a lucky number. (4) You will soon receive news regarding financial matters. (5) A settlement of legal matters. (6) A life filled with harmony and balance. (7) Good luck is coming your way when the number seven appears. (8) You will become more independent. (9) There is romance in the stars for you. (13) An unlucky number; bad luck is forthcoming.

OCTOPUS: Beware of dangerous situations ahead. It would be wise to reconsider a plan or intended project at the moment.

OWL: You will be faced with problems arising from the sickness or death of a loved one. If large dots and/or dashes are present, it indicates financial complications.

PIG: This is a symbol of good luck, abundance, high honors, and all ambitions realized.

PIPE: It is important for you to keep an open mind at all times. Avoid trouble or getting involved with other people's problems or else you may be sorry in the end.

RING: If the symbol of the ring appears on the side of the teacup, it indicates that a marriage ceremony will take place very shortly. (Look for significant initials, numbers, and/or astrological symbols.) If the ring appears on the bottom of the teacup, an engagement or wedding will be postponed.

SAW: This is a warning of an impending obstacle. Someone may be trying to interfere with your business or relationship.

SCISSORS: A bad symbol, indicating arguments resulting in separation.

SCORPION: This is a symbol of secretiveness and suspicion. Beware of jealous rivals and potentially dangerous situations. The symbol of the scorpion may also represent a person born under the astrological sign of Scorpio.

SHIP: Travel is indicated in the near future. If the symbol appears on the side of the teacup near the rim, be prepared for an unexpected journey relating to your home or business.

SKULL: An ominous symbol, usually indicating a death.

SNAKE: Beware, for the snake symbolizes enemies and minor misfortune. If it appears next to or inside of a square, the trouble can be averted.

SPIDER: Someone close to you is keeping a secret from you.

STAR: This is a symbol of peace and healing. It indicates a return to health in either a physical or spiritual sense. Your problems will be resolved and you will experience a feeling of renewal after overcoming a period of great difficulty. If the star appears in a circle, forming a pentagram, it is a favorable omen (especially for Witches and Pagans); if the pentagram appears upside down, however, it means that someone has cursed you or is using black magick to work against you.

SWORD: Be prepared to deal with problems arising both at work and at home. Complications of some sort may temporarily interfere with your plans or project.

TORNADO: Beware of impending disaster and misfortune. If dots and dashes are nearby, the possibility of financial hardship is indicated. If squares are near or touching, the misfortune may be averted.

TREE: This is a favorable omen of good health (both physically and spiritually). More than one tree indicates that a practical wish will soon come true for you.

TRIANGLE: It is time to start a new venture, especially if this symbol appears near the rim of the teacup. An upside-down triangle is an omen of bad luck.

UMBRELLA: A closed umbrella signifies that you will be temporarily unable to possess the things you desire. An open umbrella means you have a friend who will help you when you are in difficult situations.

WHEEL: This is a symbol of advancement. If the wheel appears near the rim of the teacup, you will receive some unexpected money or perhaps a salary increase.

WINDMILL: This is an indication of major business success.

Stolisomancy

Stolisomancy is the art and practice of divination by interpreting certain peculiarities of dress. For instance, accidentally wearing a shirt inside out is said to be an omen of bad luck throughout the entire day, while putting on a dress the wrong way by mistake portends that you will soon get a new dress or someone will present you with a gift. Another example of stolisomancy is: If your right shoelace becomes untied, it is believed to be an indication that someone you know is speaking kindly of you; if your left shoelace becomes untied, something ill is being said about you behind your back.

Egg Divination

The mystical art of divination by eggs (known by such names as oomantia, ooscopy, and ovamancy) dates back to ancient times, and nearly every culture has practiced it in one form or another.

Egg divination has been employed by many to determine the gender of an unborn child, and also to determine whether or not a person or animal has been cursed by the power of the evil eye.

Egg divination is quite simple to perform. Usually all that is required is an uncooked hen egg which can be obtained at a supermarket or dairy.

To determine whether or not a pregnant woman will give birth to twins, she (or her fortuneteller) should rub an egg on her belly for a few minutes and then break the egg open into a saucer. If it contains a single yolk, it indicates the birth of only one child; a double yolk indicates the birth of twins. If the yolk is spotted with blood, it is a bad omen which could indicate either a miscarriage or serious complications during childbirth.

If you have a good imagination, you can use the following method of egg divination to predict a future event or to gain the answer to a specific question: Take an uncooked hen egg and prick the top and bottom of it with a pin or needle. Allow three drops of the white of the egg to drip out into a clear drinking glass filled to the brim with cold water. Over the course of the next few hours the egg white will spread through the glass, forming symbolic shapes, letters, and/or numbers which can then be interpreted.

This ancient form of egg divination was practiced in Scotland on the eve of the old Druid new year (Samhain), in Spain on Saint John's Eve, and in England on the last day of the year.

Book Divination

Bibliomancy (or stichomancy) is the art and practice of divination by means of opening a book at random and then interpreting the first words or sentences read in a prophetic fashion.

Just about any book can be used in the art of divination; however, grimoires and collections of poetry or prose appear to be the most popular among modern book-divining Witches.

"Lots of the Saints" is a Christianized form of bibliomancy which employs the Gospels and the Holy Bible. For an answer to a specific question or to receive symbolic messages regarding future events, open a Bible to a randomly selected page while your eyes are closed. Place the index finger of your right hand anywhere on the page and then open your eyes. Whatever word or line your finger is pointing to can then be interpreted.

"Homeric Lots" and "Virgilian Lots" are two ancient forms of bibliomancy involving randomly selected passages from the written works of Homer and Virgil, respectively, which are then interpreted to reveal future events or to answer a specific personal question.

Ceromancy

Candle wax has been used in the divinations of many Witches and magicians since the Middle Ages. Two examples of this mystical art are as follows:

1. Write your question on the side of a black candle anointed with three drops of myrrh oil. Light the candle and hold it over a large piece of white paper. After some melted wax has accumulated at the top of the candle, close your eyes, ask your question thrice, and then quickly tilt the candle to spill the melted wax onto the paper. The symbolic pattern formed by the wax can then be studied for omens.

2. Pour some warm, melted wax into a container of cold water and then focus your eyes and mind on the shapes that the wax assumes, such as significant letters of the alphabet or symbolic patterns.

Also known as ceroscopy and carromancy, this form of wax divination was common at one time in Great Britain, Sweden, and Lithuania.

Geomancy

Geomancy is the art and practice of divination by tracing figures in dirt or sand, or by interpreting the symbolic patterns formed by objects (such as small stones, sticks, or seeds) which are dropped onto the ground.

A relatively modern form of geomancy is the method of divination known as the "Art of the Little Dots." It is quite simple and is performed in the following way: If you are right-handed, hold a pen or pencil in your left hand (or vice versa) over a blank piece of paper. Close your eyes, clear your mind of all distracting thoughts, and then quickly tap the tip of the writing instrument on the paper one hundred times. Open your eyes and look at the paper. You will see that a pattern has been formed by the random dots. Focus your eyes and mind upon the dot pattern until you are able to interpret its meaning.

Sortition

Sortition (also known as sortilege) is the art and practice of foretelling future events or determining the answer to a previously thought-of question by the casting of lots (usually two objects, one of which is marked with the word "yes" and the other with the word "no"), or by other chance choice. The casting of lots is perhaps the oldest form of divination known to man, and its practice is described in both Homer and in the Old Testament.

Numerous methods of lot-casting have been devised throughout the ages, and various objects (including dice, slips of paper, stones, knucklebones, and pieces of wood) have been used as lots.

The most famous of all lots were the Urim and Thummim, sacred amulets designed for divination purposes. Made from small pebbles or pieces of wood, they were carried in a small pouch inside the breastplate of the High Priests of Israel and used for the reading of oracles.

Cleromancy is another form of lot casting. It is quite similar to divination by dice, but uses small stones of different colors to draw omens.

Hydatoscopy

Hydatoscopy is the art and practice of divination by examination of rainwater. Omens are drawn from the various formations and sizes of rain puddles, and bowls of rainwater are gazed upon until clairvoyant visions appear on the surface of the water or in the mind's eye.

Ouija

The Ouija board is a popular tool of divination and a means to communicate with spiritual beings or entities beyond our plane of existence.

Although the modern Ouija as we know it was invented in the late nineteenth century, similar devices for divination and communication with spirits of the dead were in use in China long before the birth of Confucius.

There are some critics of the Ouija who claim that the board is a "dangerous toy" that can lead to demonic possession; however, if the Ouija is used correctly, certain precautions are observed, and the person operating it is in a healthy state of mind, there should be nothing to worry about.

I personally have been using a Ouija board for many years and not once have I ever experienced any serious problems as a result. I have found the Ouija to be an ideal instrument for spirit channeling, locating lost objects, divining the future, and obtaining daily guidance.

To help dispel any negative vibrations, I always anoint a black candle with amber oil or patchouli oil and light it prior to consulting the board. I also burn frankincense and myrrh in a brass burner and pray to the Goddess for Her blessings and divine protection.

The Ouija board is said to work best when two people (preferably a lady and a gentleman) operate the board together. They should be seated in comfortable chairs and facing each other with the board on their laps. Their fingertips should be placed very lightly on the message indicator, and only one question at a time should be asked out loud.

It is important that both persons concentrate deeply upon the matter in question and remain patient. Often it takes awhile before the power of the Ouija begins to take effect.

It is recommended that you use the board no more than a few hours each week. If you feel compelled for any reason to use it more often, it could be a warning signal of obsession. Never allow children to play with it, for they tend to be more impressionable than adults, which makes the risk of obsession even greater.

Never operate the board while under the influence of drugs or alcohol or if you are in an unhealthy emotional or mental state.

And most important of all, I would advise you to end your Ouija consultation immediately and put the board away if you should suddenly feel threatened in any way.

Crystal Scrying

The ancient art of crystal scrying is a form of divination popular among most modern Witches and Neo-Pagans. (I know of very few Witches who do not own at least one crystal ball.)

Crystal balls come in all sizes and colors. For scrying, I highly recommend using a clear or black one containing a minimum of air bubbles. Stands are available in all shapes and styles, ranging from simple to ornate. Prices vary, of course, depending upon the size of the crystal ball and the fanciness of the stand. A small crystal ball with a simple stand can usually be obtained for under $35, while a medium- to large-sized crystal ball with an attractive stand (especially a brass or marble one) can cost anywhere from $75 up to several hundred dollars, depending upon where you purchase them. (It's always best to shop around and compare prices before buying.)

If you cannot afford to invest in a crystal ball and you were not fortunate enough to inherit one from your dearly departed Witch grandmother, don't despair. There are many inexpensive objects that can be employed for scrying just as effectively. These include homemade magick mirrors, glass fishing floats, a bowl filled with black oil, a blot of ink, the flame of a candle, the fire in a fireplace, or just about any polished, light-reflecting object. (Incidentally, many of these things were used by seers to divine the future long before the crystal ball was devised.)

Consecrate a new crystal ball with salt and water; and then, using your athame, dedicate it as a tool of divination in the name of the Goddess. The next step is to cup the crystal ball in your hands and charge or "magnetize" it with your own psychic energies. This can easily be done by simply visualizing a white beam of light flowing from your hands and Third Eye chakra into the crystal ball. This charging ritual should be done often, especially before each scrying to "recharge" the crystal ball.

It is important to keep the crystal ball free of dust particles and fingerprints. Do not place it in direct sunlight and never use a waxy furniture polish or hot water to clean it.

To properly and safely wash your crystal ball, I recommend that you use a solution of equal parts lukewarm water and white vinegar. This will remove any accumulated dust and dirt without damaging the fragile crystal. Wipe it dry with a clean cloth or paper towel, and then polish it with a chamois.

A crystal ball should be covered by a black silk handkerchief anytime it is not in use, and you should take care to never permit any hands other than your own to touch or handle it in any way. If the crystal ball is touched or picked up by someone else and you feel that its occult vibrations have been disturbed or diminished, you will have to consecrate it all over again and then recharge it with your psychic energies.

Crystal scrying should always be performed in a quiet, undisturbed place. It may be done at any time of the day or night; however, I have personally found that the early morning and late evening hours are the ideal times for crystal gazing. It also seems that, for me at least, rainy afternoons and full moons are the times when clairvoyant powers are at their highest.

Place the crystal ball on its stand (unless it's a free-standing model with a flat bottom). Set it on a table about two feet away from you. Sit in a comfortable chair and focus your eyes and mind upon the crystal ball. It is vitally important that you are completely relaxed when you do this and that your mind is free from any negative or distracting thoughts that may interfere with your powers of concentration.

Crystal scrying is an art that often takes much practice and patience, so do not become discouraged and give up, should you be unsuccessful the first few (or dozen) times you try. The more naturally gifted with clairvoyant powers you are, the less time it will take for you to master the art.

The most commonly seen phenomena in a crystal ball, especially to novice scryers, are clouds which often take on a misty, smoky, or milky-looking appearance. The color of the clouds and the direction in which they move are highly significant:

WHITE clouds are favorable omens indicating good luck, good health, purity, and Goddess-energy.

BLACK clouds or dark-colored clouds are considered to be bad omens. It is wise to exercise extreme caution in all that you do whenever they appear in the crystal ball.

BLUE clouds are an indication that honor and praise lie ahead for you. Peace and tranquillity may also be symbolized.

RED clouds usually indicate impending dangers such as accidents, fires, or grave illnesses. Sometimes clouds of this color represent passion and sexuality. In order to make an accurate interpretation, you must take into consideration any other symbols or visions that may appear, and use your own intuitive feelings.

YELLOW clouds indicate that a trusted friend or business acquaintance will betray you.

ORANGE clouds indicate that a loss of some kind will take place in the near future.

GREEN clouds indicate financial gains and success. They may also symbolize fertility or nature.

PINK clouds indicate the presence of love or the possibility of a romantic love affair in the near future.

VIOLET clouds indicate spiritual strength, psychic growth, and enlightenment.

If the clouds move to the right in the crystal ball, it is an indication that benign spirits are present and are willing and able to guide the scryer.

If the clouds move to the left in the crystal ball, it is an indication that the spirits are unwilling or unable to guide the scryer at the present time.

If the clouds move in an upward direction in the crystal ball after a specific question has been asked, it is an indication that the answer is "yes."

If the clouds move in a downward direction in the crystal ball after a specific question has been asked, it is an indication that the answer is "no."

In addition to clouds, images (both actual and symbolic) may also appear as you gaze into the crystal ball. Images of a symbolic nature, usually combined with a significant color, tend to manifest at the right side of the crystal ball, while actual images of people, places, and things usually appear at the left side.

Love Divination

Cancellation is a simple and traditionally youthful method of love divination whereby a young lady crosses out letters in the name of her beloved that match those in her own, and then uses the popular formula of "he loves me; he loves me not" to the remaining letters to find out whether or not the gentleman she loves feels the same way about her.

If you are a woman who has received a marriage proposal from more than one man and you are undecided as to which one you should accept, perform the following divination: Write the names of your suitors on separate onions and bury them in a flowerpot or in the ground. The onion that sprouts first will contain the name of the man who will make the best husband for you.

This method of love divination (which is also known by the name of cromniomancy) also works just as effectively for men.

Oneiromancy

Oneiromancy is the scientific name for the divinatory art of interpreting dreams and nightmares. It is an ancient "science" that has been practiced in nearly every part of the world by Witches and non-Witches alike.

When properly interpreted, the images that dance in our heads while we sleep can reveal the future or warn us of impending disasters and health problems, either by actual or symbolic pictures.

The following is a simplified dream dictionary to help assist in the interpretations of your dreams. As there are thousands of dream symbols (each with its own special meaning), it would be next to impossible to list each one in this book. So I have included a list of what I feel are the symbols most commonly dreamed and their divinatory meanings.

Dream Dictionary

ACCIDENT: To dream about being involved in some sort of accident, or even witnessing one, is a warning omen that should be taken very seriously. You should be extremely careful, avoid travel in the near future, and steer clear of all potentially dangerous situations.

AIRPLANE: To dream that you are flying in an airplane indicates that you will be successful in all ventures. A turbulent flight indicates great obstacles that must be overcome before fulfillment of your desires can be attained. To dream of an airplane crash is a warning of impending disaster.

ALLEY: To dream of being in a dark alley is an indication that you could soon find yourself in a dilemma of some sort. A dead-end alley indicates a subconscious feeling of being trapped (in a relationship, job, lifestyle) with no way out.

ANGEL: To dream about seeing an angel dressed in white is an indication that you will receive an unexpected blessing in the near future. It is also a sign of spiritual protection. If the angel speaks to you in the dream, either verbally or telepathically, his or her words may contain an important hidden message. An angel descending from the heavens indicates improved health and/or a long life. An angel dressed all in black (Angel of Death) indicates serious illness, sorrowful news, or death.

APPLES: To dream about seeing or eating ripe apples that are delicious and sweet is an indication of good fortune and happiness, especially in love. To dream about eating a sour apple or seeing rotten apples that have fallen from a tree indicates failure, disappointment, quarrels, and unhappiness. To dream that someone of the opposite sex offers you an apple is a warning for you to avoid temptation.

ARREST: To dream that you are being arrested by a police officer or are being taken away to jail is an indication that you should be more cautious, otherwise you will end up in serious trouble.

BABY: To dream about a happy or laughing baby is an indication of loyal and caring friends. A sick or crying baby foretells emotional stress, illness, or disappointment. A sleeping baby symbolizes a desire to have a love mate. A nursing baby is an indication that a trusted friend or business acquaintance will soon deceive you. A baby in a carriage indicates a pleasant surprise in the near future. To dream that you are giving birth to a baby signifies fertility or wish fulfillment. To dream about adopting a baby warns that you should change your residence.

BAT: To dream a bat is an indication that you will receive some very unpleasant news in the near future.

BATHING: To dream about taking a bath is an indication that a cleansing of the body, mind, or spirit is needed. It may also indicate an expansion of your business or a home renovation in the near future. If you dream that you are bathing with other persons, it signifies that unpleasant gossip is being (or will be) spread about you. For a widow or widower, a dream of this nature could indicate a new marriage mate. Bathing in dirty water is an omen of illness. For persons who are suffering from a disease or emotional stress, to dream about bathing in clear water or in a stream signifies a recovery.

BEACH: To dream that you are at the beach indicates a need for pleasure and relaxation. You have been working too hard and should take some time out to unwind.

BED: To dream that you are sleeping in a strange bed is an indication of new opportunities. A neatly made bed symbolizes happiness and fidelity, while an unmade bed symbolizes deception. If you dream that you are making your bed, it signifies that you will soon make some new friends. If you dream about a sick friend or loved one who is lying in bed, it is an omen that their condition will worsen.

BEE: To dream that you are being stung by a bee is an indication of deception and disappointment. If bees are buzzing around flowers, it portends an improvement in your love life or an increase in business. To dream about killing a bee is a warning that an enemy will cause you great losses and possible ruin. A swarm of bees in a dream foretells an abundance of wealth.

BELLS: To dream of bells tolling is a bad omen, usually portending the passing of a friend or loved one. If you dream of church bells ringing, it indicates a wedding in the future, especially if other wedding symbols appear in the dream.

BICYCLE: To dream of riding a bicycle downhill is a warning of misfortune. To dream of riding a bicycle uphill is an omen that good fortune lies ahead for you. To dream that you fall off a bicycle while riding it indicates a subconscious fear of failure.

BIRDS: To dream of birds flying in your direction is an indication of a new friendship and/or prosperity in the days to come. To dream that birds are flying away from you indicates the loss of a friendship. To see a black-feathered bird in a dream is a bad omen foretelling misfortune, illness, or news of a death. The same meaning applies to dreams in which any kind of dead bird is present. A singing or wounded bird signifies sorrow. Birds that speak often appear in dreams to warn the dreamer to be careful about gossip. To dream of an empty bird's nest is an omen of disappointment and sorrow. A nest filled with eggs or baby birds is an omen of good luck and prosperity.

BRIDGE: To dream that you are crossing a bridge is an indication that whatever difficulties you are presently experiencing will soon be overcome. To dream of walking under a bridge indicates problems that need to be solved. Standing on a bridge symbolizes a beneficial encounter. A covered bridge symbolizes protection against enemies. To dream that you are falling from a bridge is an indication of failure of some kind.

BURIAL: To dream about attending the burial of a friend or relative is an indication that you will soon receive some bad news, especially if the burial takes place on a rainy, dismal day. To dream about attending your own burial or of being buried alive indicates frustration and a subconscious desire to escape from problems that seem overwhelming. A burial on a sunny day symbolizes either new opportunities to acquire prestige or news of a wedding. A burial that takes place at night indicates that a friend or relative will soon fall ill.

BUTTERFLY: To dream about seeing a butterfly is an indication of happiness and prosperity, and often the arrival of good news. To dream about catching a butterfly symbolizes heartbreak caused by a loved one who will prove unfaithful.

CANDLES: To dream about candles burning is an indication of good fortune, happiness, and true love. If the candles flicker or are extinguished in some way, this may be an omen of health problems in the very near future.

CASTLE: To dream about being in a castle is an indication of great wealth and prestige in the future. An old castle in a state of ruin indicates that frustration and disappointments lie ahead.

CAT: To dream about a black cat (especially if you are a Witch) is an omen of good luck. A white cat indicates a loss of some kind. A cat that scratches or bites is a warning of betrayal.

CEMETERY: To dream about being in a cemetery during daylight hours is an indication of a journey or a beneficial change about to take place. To dream about being in a cemetery at night could either indicate a strong fear of dying or a death wish. Some dream analysis books say that dreams involving cemeteries are symbolic of the past (things that are "dead and buried") while others claim they are omens of marriage (if the dreamer is a widow or widower) and also omens of bad news (often the death of a loved one).

CHURCH: To dream about being in a church indicates the exchange of wedding vows in the coming year. If the church is in the distance, the dream signifies that you are about to experience a great disappointment.

EATING: To dream about eating indicates a need or want for "spiritual nourishing." To dream that you are unable to stop eating signifies numerous worries and a dissatisfaction with your present lifestyle.

FALLING: To dream that you are falling (which is a very common dream experienced by nearly everyone at one time or another) could indicate impending disaster or a subconscious fear of failure.

FATHER: To dream about your father is an indication that you will soon be faced with an important (but difficult) decision, possibly concerning a major change in your life.

FLYING: To dream that you are flying in the air like a bird indicates a strong connection with the psychic realm. Often, dreams of flying aren't actually dreams at all, but rather astral projections.

GHOST: To dream about the ghost of your mother or father is a warning of impending disaster. To dream that a ghost speaks to you indicates deception by a friend, a serious illness, or death. A black ghost symbolizes temptation; a white ghost symbolizes consolation during times of sorrow.

HOSPITAL: To dream about being in a hospital could be an indication of either an illness which will soon strike the dreamer or a loved one, or a subconscious fear of confinement.

JOURNEY: To dream that you are embarking on a journey of some kind indicates a major change will soon take place in your relationships with friends and/or lovers.

KISSING: To dream that you are kissing your lover indicates that you will have a serious lover's quarrel; however, there will be a complete reconciliation. To dream that you are kissing a stranger indicates that you and/or your family will be disgraced by scandal. To dream that you are kissing an enemy is an indication that you should make amends with that person.

LADDER: To dream that you are climbing up a ladder indicates success through hard work and persistence. To dream that you are climbing down or falling from a ladder denotes a failure of some kind (often as the result of a bad habit or addiction).

LETTER: To dream about receiving a letter indicates that you will soon receive some unpleasant news. If the letter is in a black envelope or is written on black-bordered paper, it is an omen of death. A pink or red letter means you will receive good news from your lover. If a letter is delivered to you by a white dove; it is a good omen signifying happiness and the possibility of a new romance. To receive an anonymous letter indicates a troubled conscience.

MAGICIAN: To dream about a magician (or wizard) symbolizes a desire to obtain wisdom, power, or arcane knowledge.

MIRROR: To dream of breaking a mirror (either accidentally or deliberately) is an indication of bad luck or the death of a loved one. (The same meaning applies to a falling mirror.) To dream about seeing your lover's reflection when you look into a mirror signifies lover's quarrels and/or estrangement. To see your own reflection in a mirror (especially a cracked one) is an omen of ill health or loss of personal property either by theft or disaster.

MONEY: To dream about losing your money indicates that you will soon find some, and vice versa. To dream about stealing money is an indication that you will experience financial difficulties. According to one old superstition:

The more money you dream about, the less money you will actually have.

MOTHER: To dream about your mother indicates a subconscious need for love, protection, and nurturing. If your mother calls to you in the dream, it could signify a guilty conscience.

NUDITY: To dream about being nude and embarrassed (especially in a public place) indicates a subconscious fear of having your secrets discovered or your private life exposed.

NUMBERS: Whenever numbers appear in a dream it is an indication that they will either be very lucky or very unlucky for the dreamer. Dream numbers often hold personal significance for the person dreaming about them, such as an age, an address, a time or date, and so on.

OCEAN: To dream about a calm ocean indicates a streak of good luck or possibly a journey in the near future. A stormy ocean indicates danger, bad luck, or the beginning of a serious problem. An ocean covered with foam indicates deception. To dream that you are drowning in the ocean means a great loss of some kind will soon take place. To dream of seeing others drowning signifies protection against enemies and/or evil-natured supernatural entities.

RAIN: To dream about a light rain is an indication of good fortune and happy times to come. To dream about cold rain or sleet indicates disappointment concerning your job or career. A storm is a warning of serious problems forming in the very near future.

RUNNING: To dream that you are running or jogging is an indication of advancement. To dream that you are running away from someone or something indicates a subconscious desire to escape from your problems or responsibilities. To dream that you are stumbling while running is a warning that a new venture will turn out to be difficult or possibly unsuccessful.

SCHOOL: To dream about being back in school is an indication of frustration or a subconscious feeling that you are being examined or tested in some way.

SNAKE: To dream about seeing or handling any kind of snake indicates the presence of a powerful enemy or an obsession of some sort. To dream about being bitten by a snake signifies a betrayal by a friend, a loved one, or a trusted business acquaintance.

STAIRS: To dream about walking up a flight of stairs is an indication of good luck in the coming days. Walking down the stairs indicates the opposite. Falling down the stairs denotes obstacles in your life caused by jealous rivals or misinformation.

SWIMMING: To dream that you are swimming indicates good health and happiness. Swimming with great difficulty or being unable to keep your head above the water is a warning of danger.

TUNNEL: To dream about being lost or trapped in a dark tunnel indicates a subconscious feeling of insecurity and/or a desire to flee from problems or responsibilities. To dream about riding through a tunnel in a car or train signifies a need for sexual fulfillment.

WEDDING: To dream that you are attending a wedding indicates that a happy event will take place in your life in the near future. To dream about your own wedding, if you are single, means you will soon receive some unpleasant news. To dream about your own wedding, if you are a married person, is an indication of jealousy, marital problems, or unpleasant changes.

WITCH: To dream about a bad or ugly Witch (especially of the stereotyped Halloween variety) signifies harm caused by jealousy and/or greed, according to one dream interpretation book. To dream about a good or beautiful Witch indicates a need for the advice of a wise and experienced woman.

WOUND: To dream about being physically wounded indicates that you will be badly influenced by an evil-natured person who will come into your life in the very near future.

WREATH: To dream about seeing a festive holiday wreath on a door or fireplace is an indication of a reunion of friends and/or family members. To see a black wreath or one with a black bow is a bad omen, usually signifying a death in the family.

ZOO: To dream about visiting a zoo is an indication that others are spreading gossip about you behind your back. To dream that you are caged like an animal indicates a subconscious feeling of being trapped in an unpleasant situation or in a tiresome routine.

5

The Magickal Association of Herbs

HERBS ASSOCIATED WITH AID IN LEGAL MAT-TERS: buckthorn, High John the Conqueror, galangal.

HERBS ASSOCIATED WITH ANTI-SORCERY/UNCROSSING: absinthe, African ginger, agrimony, ague weed, angelica, anise seed, ash leaves, basil, bay, benzoin, betony, blessed thistle, blood root, boneset, broom, cinquefoil, clover, cloves, curry powder, dill, dog grass, dragon's blood, elder, fennel, flax, frankincense, galangal, gentian, geranium, ginger, hawthorn, huckleberry, hyacinth, hyssop, lilac, lotus flowers, mandrake root, marigold, marjoram, mistletoe, mugwort, nettle, peony root, pine (bark), polk root, rue, sage, Saint John's wort, sloe (berries and bark), spikenard, tormentil, unicorn root, valerian, vervain, vetivert, woodruff, wormwood.

HERBS ASSOCIATED WITH ASTRAL PROJECTION: dittany, mugwort.

HERBS ASSOCIATED WITH COURAGE: columbine, rose, thyme.

HERBS ASSOCIATED WITH DIVINATION: acacia, adder's tongue, camphor, cloves, cowslip, daisy, dandelion, fran kincense, goldenrod, hawthorn flowers, hibiscus, honeysuckle, lemon grass, mace, mugwort, nutmeg, orris root, peppermint, rose, thyme, vervain, wormwood, yarrow.

HERBS ASSOCIATED WITH DREAM MAGICK: adder's tongue, agrimony, anise, camphor, celandine (lesser), cinnamon, daisy, holly, hops, ivy, lemon verbena, mandrake root, marigold, mistletoe, mugwort, onion, peppermint, purslane, rose, Saint John's wort, verbena, vervain, wormwood, yarrow.

HERBS ASSOCIATED WITH THE EVIL EYE: figwort, garlic, hyacinth, tulip. (See also HERBS ASSOCIATED WITH PROTECTION, and HERBS ASSOCIATED WITH ANTI-SORCERY/UNCROSSING.)

HERBS ASSOCIATED WITH EXORCISM: angelica, basil, cloves, dragon's blood, elder, fern, fleabane, frankincense, garlic, horehound, juniper, lilac, mallow, mint, mistletoe, mugwort, myrrh, periwinkle, rue, Solomon's seal, Saint John's wort, thistle, vervain, yarrow.

HERBS ASSOCIATED WITH FAIRIES, ELVES, AND WOODLAND SPIRITS: daisy, elecampane (elfwort), foxglove (fairy fingers, fairy's caps, fairy's thimbles, fairy's gloves), Indian pipe (fairy smoke), ragweed (fairies' horse), ragwort, shamrock (leprechaun clover), wood sorrel.

HERBS ASSOCIATED WITH FERTILITY/VIRILITY: catnip, geranium, ginseng, lotus flowers, mandrake root, mugwort, myrtle, sarsaparilla, tansy, yohimbe.

HERBS ASSOCIATED WITH GOOD LUCK: buckthorn (bark), chamomile, clover (especially fourleaf clover), dandelion, dragon's blood, frankincense, goldenrod, heal-all, honeysuckle, huckleberry (leaves), hydrangea, Irish moss, Job's tears, John the Conqueror, kelp, khus-khus, lotus flowers, lucky hand root, mistletoe, mojo wish bean, myrrh, nutmeg, peony root, queen of the meadow, rose hips, rosemary, sacred bark, sandalwood, satyrion root, star anise, spearmint, strawberry, tonka bean, tulip.

HERBS ASSOCIATED WITH HEALTH: all-heal, allspice, asafetida, ash leaves, betony, buckeye, caraway seeds, carnation, catnip, citron, coriander, eucalyptus, feverfew, gardenia, ginseng, horehound, John the Conqueror, laurel, life-everlasting, narcissus, peppermint, rose, rue, sarsaparilla, sassafras, thyme, vervain, wintergreen.

HERBS ASSOCIATED WITH IMMORTALITY: motherwort, periwinkle, tansy.

HERBS ASSOCIATED WITH INVISIBILITY: ferns, tansy.

HERBS ASSOCIATED WITH LOVE MAGICK: absinthe, Adam and Eve root, almond, aloes, apple blossoms, archangel, ash leaves, aster, balm, basil, bay laurel, bedstraw, Beth root, birthroot, bittersweet, black snakeroot, bugleweed, burdock, cardamom, catnip, cinnamon, cinquefoil, cloves, coltsfoot, columbine, coriander, crocus, cubeb berries, cumin, daisy, damiana, deer's tongue, dill seed, dragon's blood, dulse herb, elder, elecampane, fennel seeds, feverfew, five-finger grass, gentian root, ginger, grains of paradise, groundsel, heart's ease, hemp (seeds), hibiscus, hyacinth, Indian paintbrush, jasmine, juniper (berries), khus-khus, lady's mantle, laurel, lavender, lemon, licorice stick herb, lime, linden, lotus, lovage, magnolia, maidenhair fern, mandrake, marjoram, mint, mistletoe, motherwort, mullein (leaves), myrrh, myrtle, orange blossoms, orchid, orris root, passion flower, patchouli, pennyroyal, periwinkle, primrose, quassia chips, Queen Elizabeth root, raspberry, rose, rose geranium, rosemary, rue, sage, satyrion root, skullcap, senna pods, snakeroot, southernwood, spikenard, strawberry, sweet bugle, thyme, vanilla, verbena (root), vervain, vetivert, violet, wormwood, yerba mate, ylang ylang.

HERBS ASSOCIATED WITH LUNAR MAGICK: acanthus, adder's tongue, African daisy, anise, cabbage, calla lily, chickweed, clary sage, cleavers, colewort, cress (water), dog rose, dog-tooth violet, duckweed, flag, ginger, goose grass, iris, jasmine, lady's smock, lettuce, loosestrife, moonwort, mugwort, opium poppy, orach, orpine, orris root, pearl trefoil, privet, purslane, rose (white), rushes, sea holly, seaweed, sesame, stonecrop, sweet flag, water chestnut, water cress, water lily, water mosses, wintergreen.

HERBS ASSOCIATED WITH MONEY SPELLS: acacia, alfalfa, almond, basil, bayberry, birthroot, bistort, buckeye, cascara sagrada, chamomile, cinnamon, clover, comfrey, dragon's blood, fenugreek, galangal, garlic, ginseng, goldenrod, High John the Conqueror, honeysuckle, Irish moss, knotweed, lavender, lovage, luckyhand root, mandrake, mountain laurel, myrtle, nutmeg, periwinkle, queen of the meadow, red clover, skullcap, sea lettuce, smartweed, snakeroot, spikenard, squill, thyme, tonka beans, tulip, vervain, yellow dock.

HERBS ASSOCIATED WITH PEACE: crocus, lotus flowers, olive branch.

HERBS ASSOCIATED WITH PROTECTION: Aaron's rod, African ginger, alfalfa, angelica, ash tree leaves, Balm of Gilead, basil, bay leaves, benzoin, bergamot, betony, black cohosh, bladderwrack, bloodroot, boldo leaves, bugleweed, burdock, calendula, caraway seeds, castor bean, cinquefoil, cloves, coltsfoot, comfrey root, cypress, dog grass, elder (berries and wood), eucalyptus, fennel seeds, flax, fleabane, four-leaf clover, foxglove, gardenia, garlic, heather, holy ghost root, holy herb, horehound, Indian turnip, iris, Irish moss, John the Conqueror, kava kava, knotweed, lilac, lily of the valley, lovage, marjoram, mint, mistletoe, motherwort, mugwort, mullein, mustard seed, patchouli, peony root, periwinkle, purslane, quince, ragwort, raspberry, rose geranium, rowan tree (leaves and blossoms), Saint John's wort, sandalwood, Solomon's seal, spikenard, stone root, tansy, vervain, vetivert, woodruff, wormwood, yarrow.

HERBS ASSOCIATED WITH PSYCHIC DEVELOPMENT: absinthe, acacia (flowers), African ginger, anise seeds, bladderwrack, calendula, camphor, cinnamon, cloves, dandelion, four-leaf clover, frankincense, gum mastic, heliotrope, honeysuckle, hyssop, kava kava, laurel, lavender, lilac, linseed, magnolia, mandrake, mugwort, mullein, orchid, peppermint, purslane, queen root, rosemary, saffron, thyme, wisteria, wood rose, yarrow.

HERBS ASSOCIATED WITH SHAPE-SHIFTING: catnip, centaury, mandrake root, morning glory (seeds), peyote, wolfsbane.

HERBS ASSOCIATED WITH SORCERY (THE BLACK ARTS): balmony, barberry, belladonna, black pepper, blood root, blueberry (leaves), boneset, chicory, deadly nightshade, hellebore, hemlock, henbane, jimsonweed, knot grass, lemon verbena, lobelia, mandrake, mullein, patchouli, poison hemlock, pokeweed, red pepper, saffron, skunk cabbage, slippery elm, snake root, sumac, tormentil, valerian, willow (bark), Witch grass, wolfsbane, yarrow.

HERBS ASSOCIATED WITH SPIRIT CONJURATIONS: African ginger, althea, anise, bladderwrack, carnation, dittany, foxglove, frankincense, gardenia, heather, lemon verbena, lime, lotus flowers, mandrake, thyme, violet, wintergreen, wormwood.

HERBS ASSOCIATED WITH SPIRITUAL HEALING: angelica, bay, carnation, cedar, cinnamon, fennel, feverfew, frankincense, gardenia, geranium, groundsel, hops, horehound, juniper, lemon balm, lotus flowers, mint, motherwort, myrrh, peppermint, rose, rosemary, sandalwood, thyme, vervain, violet, willow, wood sorrel, yerba santa.

HERBS ASSOCIATED WITH SPIRITUAL PURIFICATION: avens, cloves, fennel seeds, frankincense, garlic, ginseng, myrrh, rosemary, sage.

HERBS ASSOCIATED WITH SUCCESS: basil, bergamot, blue flag, frankincense, grains of paradise, lemon verbena, mistletoe, myrrh, sandalwood, Solomon's seal, squill (root), storax, vanilla, yellow dock.

HERBS ASSOCIATED WITH WEATHERWORKING: ferns, heather, houseleek, mugwort, Saint John's wort, Solomon's seal, witch hazel.

HERBS ASSOCIATED WITH WISDOM: iris, mulberry.

HERBS ASSOCIATED WITH WISH-MAGICK: lucky hand root, satyrion root, vervain, violet.

HERBS ASSOCIATED WITH WITCHCRAFT AND MAGICK: angelica, belladonna, foxglove (Witches' bells, Witches' gloves), frankincense, ginseng, heather (Witches' broom), hemlock, henbane, mandrake root, mugwort, mullein (Witches' candle), myrrh, periwinkle (sorcerer's violet), poison hemlock (warlock weed), Saint John's wort, Solomon's seal, vervain (enchanter's plant, Witchwort), Witch grass, yarrow.

6

The Sabbats

The Sabbat is a traditional seasonal holiday celebrating the "wheel" of birth-death-rebirth, made possible by the sacred union of the Fertility-Goddess and Her consort, the Horned God.

A total of eight different Sabbats (four major and four minor) are celebrated by Wiccan covens and solitaries during the course of a year.

All Sabbats are times to celebrate Nature, dance, sing, feast, and pay homage to the old Pagan gods; however, each individual Sabbat has its own traditional herbs, incense, candle colors, gemstones, and so on.

The Four Major Sabbats

CANDELMAS SABBAT (also know as Imbolc, Oimelc, and Lady Day) is celebrated on February 2.

BELTANE SABBAT (also known as May Day, Rood Day, Rudemas, and Walpurgisnacht) is celebrated on May Eve and May 1.

LAMMAS SABBAT (also known as Lughnasadh, August Eve, and the First Festival of Harvest) is celebrated on August 1.

SAMHAIN (also known as Halloween, Hallowmas, All Hallows' Eve, All Saint's Eve, Festival of the Dead, and the Third Festival of Harvest) is celebrated on October 31.

The Four Minor Sabbats

SPRING EQUINOX SABBAT (also known as Vernal Equinox Sabbat, Festival of the Trees, Alban Eilir, Ostara, and Rite of Eostre) is celebrated on the first day of Spring.

SUMMER SOLSTICE SABBAT (also know as Midsummer, Alban Hefin, and Litha) is celebrated on the first day of Summer.

AUTUMN EQUINOX SABBAT (also known as the Fall Sabbat, Alban Elfed, and the Second Festival of Harvest) is celebrated on the first day of Fall.

WINTER SOLSTICE SABBAT (also known as Yule, Winter Rite, Midwinter, and Alban Arthan) is celebrated on the first day of Winter.

Traditional Pagan Foods of the Sabbats

CANDLEMAS: Foods that represent growth, such as seeds (pumpkin, sesame, sunflower, etc.), poppyseed breads and cakes, and herbal teas.

SPRING EQUINOX: Hard-boiled eggs (to symbolize fertility), honey cakes, the first fruits of the season, waffles, and milk punch.

BELTANE: All red fruits (such as strawberries and cherries), green herbal salads, red or pink wine punch, and large, round oatmeal or barley cakes known as "Beltane Cakes."

SUMMER SOLSTICE: Fresh vegetables, summer fruits, pumpernickel bread, ale, and mead.

LAMMAS: Homemade breads (wheat, oat, and especially corn bread), barley cakes, nuts, wild berries, apples, rice, roasted lamb, berry pies, elderberry wine, ale, and meadowsweet tea.

AUTUMN EQUINOX: Corn and wheat products, breads, nuts, vegetables, apples, roots (carrots, onions, potatoes, etc.), cider, and pomegranates.

SAMHAIN: Apples, pumpkin pie, hazelnuts, Cakes for the Dead, corn, cranberry muffins and breads, ale, cider, and herbal teas (especially mugwort).

WINTER SOLSTICE: Roasted turkey, nuts, fruitcakes, caraway rolls, eggnog, and mulled wine.

Traditional Ritual Herbs of the Sabbats

CANDLEMAS: angelica, basil, bay, benzoin, celandine, heather, myrrh, and all yellow flowers.

SPRING EQUINOX: acorn, celandine, cinquefoil, crocus, daffodil, dogwood, Easter lily, honeysuckle, iris, jasmine, rose, strawberry, tansy, and violets.

BELTANE: almond, angelica, ash tree, bluebells, cinquefoil, daisy, frankincense, hawthorn, ivy, lilac, marigold, meadowsweet, primrose, roses, satyrion root, woodruff, and yellow cowslips.

SUMMER SOLSTICE: chamomile, cinquefoil, elder, fennel, hemp, larkspur, lavender, male fern, mugwort, pine, roses, Saint John's wort, wild thyme, wisteria, and verbena.

LAMMAS: acacia flowers, aloes, cornstalks, cyclamen, fenugreek, frankincense, heather, hollyhock, myrtle, oak leaves, sunflower, and wheat.

AUTUMN EQUINOX: acorns, asters, benzoin, ferns, honeysuckle, marigold, milkweed, mums, myrrh, oak leaves, passionflower, pine, roses, sage, Solomon's seal, and thistles.

SAMHAIN: acorns, apples, broom, deadly nightshade, dittany, ferns, flax, fumitory, heather, mandrake, mullein, oak leaves, sage, and straw.

WINTER SOLSTICE: bay, bayberry, blessed thistle, cedar, chamomile, evergreen, frankincense, holly, juniper, mistletoe, moss, oak, pine cones, rosemary, and sage.

Sabbat Altar Decorations

CANDLEMAS: a crown of thirteen red candles, a spring of evergreen, a besom or Witch's broom to symbolize the "sweeping out of the old," a small statue or figurine representing the Triple Goddess in Her Maiden aspect.

SPRING EQUINOX: hard-boiled eggs colored and painted with magickal symbols to symbolize fertility, a lucky rabbit's foot amulet, a bowl of green and yellow jellybeans.

BELTANE: a small Maypole and/or a phallus-shaped candle to symbolize fertility, a daisy chain, springtime wildflowers (such as primrose, yellow cowslips, or marigolds).

SUMMER SOLSTICE: summertime flowers, love amulets, seashells, aromatic potpourri, summer fruits.

LAMMAS: corn dollies (small figures fashioned from braided straw) and/or kirn babies (corncob dolls) to symbolize the Mother Goddess of the Harvest.

AUTUMN EQUINOX: acorns, pinecones, autumn leaves, a pomegranate to symbolize Persephone's descent into the Underworld, a small statue or figure representing the Triple Goddess in Her Mother aspect.

SAMHAIN: a jack-o'-lantern, apples, candles in the shapes of Witches, ghosts, black cats, skulls, photographs of deceased loved ones, tools of divination, a small statue or figure representing the Triple Goddess in Her Crone aspect.

WINTER SOLSTICE: mistletoe, holly, a small Yule log, strings of colored lights, Yule/Christmas cards, a candle in the shape of Kriss Kringle (Santa Claus), presents wrapped in colorful holiday paper, a homemade wreath.

Sabbat Incense

CANDLEMAS: basil, myrrh, and wisteria.

SPRING EQUINOX: African violet, jasmine, rose, sage, and strawberry.

BELTANE: frankincense, lilac, and rose.

SUMMER SOLSTICE: frankincense, lemon, myrrh, pine, rose, and wisteria.

LAMMAS: aloes, rose, and sandalwood.

AUTUMN EQUINOX: benzoin, myrrh, and sage.

SAMHAIN: apple, heliotrope, mint, nutmeg, and sage.

WINTER SOLSTICE: bayberry, cedar, pine, and rosemary.

Sacred Sabbat Gemstones

CANDLEMAS: amethyst, garnet, onyx, turquoise.

SPRING EQUINOX: amethyst, aquamarine, bloodstone, red jasper.

BELTANE: emerald, orange carnelian, sapphire, rose quartz.

SUMMER SOLSTICE: all green gemstones, especially emerald and jade.

LAMMAS: aventurine, citrine, peridot, sardonyx.

AUTUMN EQUINOX: carnelian, lapis lazuli, sapphire, yellow agate.

SAMHAIN: all black gemstones, especially jet, obsidian, and onyx.

WINTER SOLSTICE: cat's-eye and ruby.

Sabbat Deities

CANDLEMAS: The Goddess in Her aspect as the Maiden, Brigid (Celtic goddess of fire, wisdom, poetry, and sacred wells; also a deity associated with prophecy, divination, and healing), and Aradia (daughter of Diana, and "founder of the Witch cult on Earth").

SPRING EQUINOX: Eostre (Saxon goddess of fertility), Ostara (German goddess of fertility), the Green Goddess, and Lord of the Greenwood.

BELTANE: Flora (Roman flower-goddess), the lunar goddesses Diana and Artemis, Pan (the Greek horned goat-god of woodlands, fields, shepherds, and fertility), Faunus (the Roman equivalent to Pan), and all fertility deities.

SUMMER SOLSTICE: Aphrodite, Astarte, Freya, Hathor, Ishtar, Venus, and other goddesses who preside over love, passion, and beauty.

LAMMAS: Lugh (a Celtic solar deity worshipped by the ancient Druids), John Barleycorn (the personification of malt liquor), Demeter, Ceres, the Corn Mother, and other goddesses who preside over agriculture.

AUTUMN EQUINOX: The Goddess in Her aspect of the Mother, Persephone (Queen of the Underworld), and Thor (Lord of thunder in Norse mythology).

SAMHAIN: The Goddess in Her dark aspect as the Crone, Hecate (goddess of fertility and moon-magick, and protectress of all Witches), Morrigan (Celtic goddess of death), Cernunnos (Celtic fertility god), and Osiris (an ancient Egyptian deity whose annual death and rebirth personified the self-renewing vitality and fertility of Nature).

WINTER SOLSTICE: Lucina (Roman goddess of lunar mysteries), Frey (Scandinavian god of fertility and a deity associated with peace and prosperity), Attis (Phrygian fertility god), Dionysus (Greek god of wine), Woden (the chief Teutonic god), and, of course, jolly old Kriss Kringle (the Pagan god of Yule and personification of the Yuletide spirit).

Sabbat Candle Colors

CANDLEMAS: white, red, pink, brown.

SPRING EQUINOX: green, yellow, gold, and all pastel shades.

BELTANE: dark green and colors of the rainbow spectrum.

SUMMER SOLSTICE: blue, green, yellow.

LAMMAS: golden yellow, orange, green, light brown.

AUTUMN EQUINOX: orange, dark red, yellow, indigo, brown.

SAMHAIN: black, orange.

WINTER SOLSTICE: red, green, white, gold, silver.

Sabbat Potpourri

A small cauldron filled with homemade potpourri can be used as a fragrant altar decoration, burned (outdoors) as an offering to the old gods during or after a Sabbat celebration, or wrapped in decorative paper and ribbons and given to a Wiccan sister or brother as a Sabbat gift.

CANDLEMAS RITUAL POTPOURRI

45 drops myrrh oil
1 cup oak moss
2 cups dried heather flowers
2 cups dried wisteria
1 cup dried yellow tulip petals
1/2 cup dried basil
1/2 cup dried and chopped bay leaves

Mix the myrrh oil with the oak moss, and then add the remaining ingredients. Stir the potpourri well and then store in a tightly covered ceramic or glass container.

SPRING EQUINOX RITUAL POTPOURRI

45 drops rose oil
1 cup oak moss
2 cups dried dogwood blossoms
2 cups dried honeysuckle blossoms
1/2 cup dried violets
1/2 cup dried daffodils
1/2 cup dried rosebuds
1/2 cup dried crocus or iris

Mix the rose oil with the oak moss, and then add the remaining ingredients. Stir the potpourri well and then store in a tightly covered ceramic or glass container.

BELTANE RITUAL POTPOURRI

45 drops frankincense oil
1 cup oak moss
1 cup dried bluebells
1 cup dried lilac
1 cup dried marigold
1 cup dried meadowsweet
1 cup dried rosebuds and petals
1 cup dried yellow cowslips

Mix the frankincense oil with the oak moss and then add the remaining ingredients. Stir the potpourri well and store in a tightly covered ceramic or glass container.

SUMMER SOLSTICE RITUAL POTPOURRI

45 drops lemon or lavender oil
1 cup oak moss
2 cups dried lavender
2 cups dried wisteria
2 cups dried verbena

Mix the lemon or lavender oil with the oak moss, and then add the remaining ingredients. Stir the potpourri well and store in a tightly covered ceramic or glass container.

LAMMAS RITUAL POTPOURRI

20 drops clove bud oil
25 drops sandalwood oil
1 cup oak moss
2 cups dried pink rosebuds
2 cups dried red peony petals
1 cup dried amaranth flowers
1 cup dried heather flowers
½ cup dried cornflowers

Mix the clove bud and sandalwood oils with the oak moss and then add the remaining ingredients. Stir the potpourri well and store in a tightly covered ceramic or glass container.

AUTUMN EQUINOX RITUAL POTPOURRI

45 drops honeysuckle oil
1 cup oak moss
6 small acorns
2 cups dried oak leaves
2 cups dried honeysuckle
1 cup dried passionflower
1 cup dried rosebuds and petals
½ cup dried pine needles
1 tablespoon sage

Mix the honeysuckle oil with the oak moss and then add the remaining ingredients. Stir the potpourri well and store in a tightly covered ceramic or glass container.

SAMHAIN RITUAL POTPOURRI

45 drops patchouli oil
1 cup oak moss
2 cups dried apple blossoms
2 cups dried heather flowers
1 cup dried and chopped apple peel
1 cup dried pumpkin seeds
½ cup dried and chopped mandrake root

Mix the patchouli oil with the oak moss, and then add the remaining ingredients. Stir the potpourri well and store in a tightly covered ceramic or glass container.

WINTER SOLSTICE RITUAL POTPOURRI

20 drops musk oil
25 drops pine oil
1 cup oak moss
2 cups dried mistletoe
1 cup dried poinsettia flowers
1 cup dried bayberries
½ cup dried rosemary
½ cup dried holly leaves and berries
3 crushed pinecones

Mix the musk and pine oils with the oak moss, and then add the remaining ingredients. Stir the potpourri well and store in a tightly covered ceramic or glass container

7

The Magickal Cookbook

BEWITCHING BROWNIES

1 cup shortening
4 (1-ounce) squares unsweetened chocolate
2 cups sugar
3 tablespoons dark rum
4 eggs, beaten
1 teaspoon vanilla extract
1½ cup flour
½ teaspoon salt
¾ cup chopped walnuts or pecans

Melt the shortening and chocolate in top of a double boiler over simmering water. Remove from heat and add the sugar and rum, mixing well. Add the eggs and vanilla extract and beat until well blended. Stir in the flour and salt, and then fold in the chopped nuts.

Spread the batter evenly in a well-greased 13 × 9 × 2-inch baking pan. Bake for 25 minutes in a 350-degree preheated oven. Cool completely in pan, frost with your favorite chocolate or vanilla frosting (if desired), and then cut the brownies into squares or bars and enjoy. (This recipe yields about 1½ dozen 3 × 2-inch brownie bars.)

CANDELMAS CRESCENT CAKES

1¼ cups flour
¾ cup sugar
1 cup finely ground almonds
3 drops almond extract
½ cup butter or margarine, softened
1 tablespoon honey
1 egg yolk

In a large mixing bowl, combine the first four ingredients. Add the butter, honey, and egg yolk and mix together well. Cover with aluminum foil or plastic wrap, and then chill for 1½ to 2 hours in the refrigerator.

When ready, pinch off pieces of the dough (about the size of plums) and shape them into crescents.

Place the crescents on a well-greased cookie sheet and bake in a 325-degree preheated oven for approximately 20 minutes. (This recipe yields about one dozen Candlemas Crescent Cakes.)

CAULDRON COOKIES

3/4 cup softened butter
2 cups brown sugar
2 eggs
1 tablespoon lemon juice
2 teaspoons grated lemon rind
2 cups flour
1 cup finely chopped pecans

Cream the butter in a large cast-iron cauldron (or mixing bowl). Gradually add the brown sugar, beating well. Add the eggs, lemon juice, and rind, and then beat by hand or with an electric mixer until the mixture is well blended. The next step is to stir in the flour and pecans.

Cover the cauldron with a lid, aluminum foil, or plastic wrap, and refrigerate overnight.

When ready, shape the dough into one-inch balls and place them about three inches apart on greased cookie sheets. Bake in a 375-degree preheated oven for approximately eight minutes. Remove from the oven and place on wire racks until completely cool.

This recipe yields about 36 cookies which can be served at any of the eight Sabbats, as well as at Esbats and all other Witchy get-togethers.

COUNTRY-WITCH EGGNOG RECIPE

1 cup apple cider
3 cups milk
2 eggs, beaten
1/2 cup whipping cream
1/2 cup sugar
1/2 teaspoon cinnamon
1/4 teaspoon ground nutmeg
2 tablespoons brandy

Combine all of the ingredients in a large cauldron or pot and cook over medium heat for 13 minutes. Pour the hot eggnog into mugs and top each serving with fresh whipped cream (if desired).

Country-Witch Eggnog is the perfect drink to serve your Wiccan friends and family members at Yuletide (Winter Solstice) and Ostara (Spring Equinox) sabbats. (This recipe yields two quarts.)

COVENSTEAD BREAD

³/₄ cup water
¹/₂ cup honey
¹/₂ cup finely chopped citron
¹/₂ cup sugar
2 tablespoons anise seeds
2¹/₃ cups flour
1¹/₂ teaspoons baking soda
1 teaspoon nutmeg
1 teaspoon cinnamon
¹/₄ teaspoon allspice

Bring the water to a boil in a saucepan. Add honey, citron, sugar, and anise seeds. Stir until the sugar completely dissolves and then remove from heat.

Sift together flour, baking soda, salt, and spices, and fold into the hot honey mixture. Turn the batter into a well-greased 9 × 5 × 3-inch loaf pan and bake in a preheated 350-degree oven for one hour. Turn out on a wire rack to cool. (This recipe yields one loaf of bread.)

Convenstead Bread improves if allowed to stand for a day, and it is an ideal bread to serve during Lammas and Autumn Equinox Sabbats as well as at all coven meetings.

GINGERBREAD WITCHES

$^1/_2$ cup softened butter
$^1/_2$ cup brown sugar
2 teaspoons ground ginger
2 teaspoons cinnamon
$^1/_2$ teaspoon allspice
$^1/_2$ teaspoon salt
$^1/_2$ cup molasses
1 egg
$3^1/_2$ cups flour
1 teaspoon baking soda
$^1/_2$ teaspoon baking powder
raisins

In a large mixing bowl, cream together the butter, brown sugar, ginger, cinnamon, allspice, and salt. Beat in the molasses and egg.

In another bowl, combine the flour, baking soda, and baking powder, mixing well. Add to the molasses mixture and stir until smooth.

Divide the dough into four equal parts. Cover with aluminum foil or plastic wrap, and then chill for $1^1/_2$ to 2 hours in the refrigerator.

When ready, roll each quarter to $^1/_4$-inch thickness on a lightly floured surface with a floured rolling pin. Cut the dough with a Witch-shaped cookie cutter (or other Halloween-theme cutters such as pumpkins, bats, skulls, etc.) Press raisins into the dough to make eyes, mouth, buttons, and so on.

Place the gingerbread Witches on a greased cookie sheet and bake in a 350-degree preheated oven for eight to ten minutes or until golden brown. Remove from the oven and place on wire racks to cool. Decorate the cookies with black and orange colored icing if desired.

This recipe yields about 30 cookies.

HALLOWEEN PUMPKIN MUFFINS

4 cups flour
3 cups sugar
1³/₄ teaspoons baking soda
1 teaspoon salt
¹/₂ teaspoon baking powder
1 tablespoon ground cloves
1 tablespoon cinnamon
1 tablespoon nutmeg
¹/₂ tablespoon ginger
1¹/₂ cups raisins
¹/₂ cup walnuts (chopped)
4 eggs
2¹/₂ cups mashed cooked pumpkin
1 cup vegetable oil
1 cup water

In a large mixing bowl, combine the first eleven ingredients, and then make a "well" in the middle of the mixture. In a separate bowl, beat the eggs lightly and then add the pumpkin, vegetable oil, and water. Mix together well. Add the egg mixture to the dry ingredients and stir just until moistened. (Do not overstir!)

Spoon into paper-lined muffin pans, filling about two-thirds full. Bake for 20 minutes in a preheated 375-degree oven and then immediately remove the muffins from the pans to prevent them from scorching and drying out. (This recipe yields about 3¹/₂ dozen muffins.)

MIDSUMMER RITUAL MEAD

2½ gallons water (preferably fresh rainwater blessed by a
    Wiccan priestess or priest)
1 cup meadowsweet herb
1 cup woodruff sprigs
1 cup heather flowers
3 cloves
1 cup honey
¼ cup brown sugar
1 cup barley malt
1 oz. brewer's yeast

Pour the water into a large cauldron or kettle. Bring to a boil
and add the meadowsweet herb, woodruff sprigs, heather
flowers, and cloves. Boil for one hour and then add the
honey, brown sugar, and barley malt. Stir thirteen times in a
clockwise direction and then remove from heat.

Strain through a cheesecloth and allow the mead to cool
to room temperature. Stir in the brewer's yeast. Cover with a
clean towel and let it stand for one day and one night. Strain
again, bottle, and then store in a cool place until ready to
serve.

Midsummer Ritual Mead is an ideal drink to serve at
Summer Solstice Sabbats, as well as during all Cakes and Ale
Ceremonies and Esbats.

SALEM WITCH PUDDING

4 eggs, separated
1½ cups pumpkin purée
1 cup light brown sugar
¾ cup half-and-half
5 tablespoons rum
½ teaspoon ground cloves
½ teaspoon ground ginger
½ teaspoon ground nutmeg
¼ teaspoon salt

In an electric mixer or large mixing bowl, beat the egg whites until stiff. In a different bowl, beat the egg yolks until thick and lemon-colored. Combine the yolks with the remaining eight ingredients; mix together well; and then fold in the egg whites.

Pour the pumpkin mixture into a buttered 1-quart soufflé dish. Place it in a pan of hot water and bake in a 350-degree preheated oven for about 45 minutes. (This recipe yields 6 servings.)

8

Pagan Resources

ABYSS DISTRIBUTION
48-GIP Chester Road
Chester, MA 01011
(413) 623-2155
Free occult catalogue! Over 2,400 books, plus 5,000 other ritual items. Amulets, jewelry, herbs, perfumes, incense, burners, candles, statues, and more. Magickal one-stop shopping. Retail/wholesale.

AMULETS BY MERLIN
P. O. Box 2643
Newport News, VA 23609
A complete line of original design jewelry and hand engraving. We specialize in custom design work for groups or individuals in silver, bronze, and gold. Also available, a one-of-a-kind Tarot Casting Set: the result of 13 years of research. This set encompasses the Tarot, Qabalahistic, and astrologi-

cal correlation in each amulet; resulting in a revolutionary form of divination. Catalogue: $1.00

ANCIENT CIRCLES/OPEN CIRCLE
P. O. Box 610
Laytonville, CA 95451
1-800-726-8032
Symbolic jewelry of Celtic design, pendants in Goddess and God images, temple formula perfumes and other such items. Some of the "new classics" are exclusively by us—the Celtic Pentagram, Bamburg Green Man, and more! Catalogue: $2.00

THE BEAD TREE
Box 682
West Falmouth, MA 02574
(508) 548-4665
Earrings and/or pendants taken from ancient images of the Goddess. Medicine card earrings and/or pendant with your totem animal and other charms. All contain symbols of Earth, Air, Fire, and Water. Send $1.00 for brochures.

COMING OUT PAGAN
Quarterly newsletter for LesBiGay pagans of all traditions. High-quality publication with an international readership. Networking, community resources, media reviews, fiction, poetry, tarot, humor, and more! Artwork and short written submissions welcome. Confidentiality assured. Subscribers receive a FREE 40-word classified ad. Subscriptions: U.S. $11, Canada $13, Overseas $15. Sample issue $3. Please make all checks or money orders (U.S. funds only, please) to: Wordsmith Writing Services, P. O. Box 30811, Bethesda, MD 20824-0811

COSMIC VISION LTD
(formerly *THE OCCULT EMPORIUM*)

956 Hamilton Street
Allentown, PA 18102
(610) 433-3610
Ancient Wisdom Archive & Supply—Retail & mail-order illustrated catalogue: $2.00. Books, herbs, incense, jewelry, minerals, candles, altar attire and equipment, brasses, tarot, consultations, magick-on-contract, experts in right/left traditions. Oils, powders, antiques, arcane specialties. U.F.O. museum on premises. Open Monday–Friday, 11:00 A.M. to 6:00 P.M., Saturday 11:00 A.M. to 5:00 P.M. Since 1975!

COVEN GARDENS
P. O. Box 1064
Boulder, CO 80306
(303) 444-4322
Occult supplies: incense, oils, bath products, herbs, candles, and more. Western Traditional ancient recipes, Wicca, Druidic/Celtic, Egyptian, Greco-Roman, Middle and Near Eastern, Macumba, and Voodoo (upon request). All planetary and Zodiacal blends are Qabalistic. Supplies to aid practitioners from Paganism to High Ceremonial ritual work. All products are made by planetary placements, lunar cycle phase, and during ritual circle.

EDEN WITHIN
P. O. Box 667
Jamestown, NY 14701
(716) 487-2839
Need ONE place to supply your every magickal need? This extensive Wiccan catalogue was started by a Wiccan who understood your frustrations of searching through several sources to get magickal items. We offer FREE GIFTS in every issue, and many items are handmade by caring hands. You'll find books, oils, jewelry, robes, chalices, statues, and much more. Why go anywhere else? Catalogue: $2.00 (refundable).

EARTH CIRCLE NEWS
P. O. Box 1938
Sebastopol, CA 95473
(707) 829-8586
A beautiful 20-page quarterly devoted to issues of interest to the circling community—Wiccan, Pagan, women's and men's circles and lodges, drumming and healing circles, new and full-moon groups—in short, nonhierarchical, Earth-centered Spirit groups that gather with an intent to heal and celebrate this earthly existence. One-year subscription: $15.00. A free back-issue sample is sent on request.

GOLDEN ISIS PRESS
Gerina Dunwich, Editor
P. O. Box 525
Fort Covington, NY 12937
Publisher of *Golden Isis* magazine (ISSN 1068-2457), a quarterly newsletter/journal of Goddess-inspired poetry, Pagan art, Wiccan news, book reviews, ads, and more. Sample copy: $2.95; one-year subscription: $10 (Canada & Overseas: $15). Also from Golden Isis Press: Tarot and Gypsy-Witch card readings, reasonably priced natal charts, past-life readings, dream interpretations, spellcasting services, *Circle of Shadows* by Gerina Dunwich, and much more! Please send a self-addressed stamped envelope and $1.00 for more information.

GYPSY HEAVEN
115 South Main Street
New Hope, Pa 18938
(215) 862-5251
The Witch Shop of New Hope! Specializing in books, herbs, oils, incense, and much more! Mail-order catalogue: $3.00 (refundable with first order).

GYPSY MOON
1780 Massachusetts Avenue (Dept. GI)

Cambridge, MA 02140

Our clothes exist for special people who feel as though they were born to another age. Our styles are transformative, designed to flow as you move. Clothing that is magic you can take with you into the larger world where magic is sorely lacking. Catalogue: $2.00.

THE HENGE OF KELTRIA
P.O. Box 33284-W
Minneapolis, MN 55433

A Neo-Pagan Druid organization that promotes Druidic education and fellowship through various journals, publications, and membership. It publishes a quarterly journal, *Keltria: Journal of Druidism and Celtic Magick,* plus *Serpent Stone: A Journal of Druidic Wisdoms,* and several other publications. For information concerning The Henge and current prices, send a self-addressed stamped envelope (#10).

INTERNATIONAL GUILD OF OCCULT SCIENCES RESEARCH SOCIETY
255 E1 Cielo Road
Suite X565X
Palm Springs, CA 92262
(619) 327-7355

Huge catalogue of rare books, courses, and products, psionic helmet and boxes, Witchcraft Radionics, time travel, hidden technology, alchemical money boxes, exorcism, PSI warfare, invisibility. Teacher, researchers, publishers, memberships available, bimonthly magazine and more! Send $3.00 for complete information and catalogue.

JOAN TERESA POWER PRODUCTS
P. O. Box 442
Mars Hill, NC 28754

Large selection of herbs, handmade fine quality oils, incense, powders and baths, candles, books, jewelry, etc. Lessons written and personal instruction. Ten percent discount all Wicca. Catalogue: $2.00.

LUNATRIX
P. O. Box 800482
Santa Clarita, CA 91380-0482
We offer a free mail-order catalogue featuring ritual items, Goddess jewelry, T-shirts, incense, oils, herbs, rubber stamps, and more! SASE please.

MARAH
Box 948
Madison, NJ 07940
Top-quality incenses, perfumes, bath salts, massage oils, and lotions for ritual and mundane purposes, personally hand-blended by Marah. Also lunar almanacs, calendars, Wicca course, herbal, and other magickal, Goddess-oriented books. Complete catalogue of all these products, plus hand-dipped candles, herbs, and other spiritual supplies. For catalogue, incense sample, and complimentary issue of Marah's Alma-nac, send $1.00.

MYSTICAL SWAN PRODUCTS
by GOLDFOX, INC.
P. O. Box 726
Forest, VA 24551
We are a small New Age company dedicated to serving the Wiccan, Pagan, and eclectic occult communities. Specializ-ing in herbal, instructional, and ritual-oriented supplies and products. Thousands to choose from. Catalogue: $2.00 (dis-counted from first order). Blessed Be!!!

NEW AGE BOOKS & THINGS, INC.
4401 North Federal Highway

Fort Lauderdale, FL 33308
(305) 771-0026
The oldest and finest metaphysical and Wiccan source for books, cards, jewelry, audio and video self-hypnosis cassettes, New Age music, incense and burners, altar supplies, candles, and information network in south Florida.

NUIT UNLIMITED
249 North Brand Blvd. (482)
Glendale, CA 91203
(213) 258-5734
Abundances of magickally charged, sensual and practical products honoring all paths for ceremonial and personal work are offered in this informative, unique mail-order catalogue. Oils from A–Z; stick and powder incense; massage oil blends; bath salts; formulations for Wiccan, Qabalistic and special purposes; ceremonial, meditation, and tantric tapes; statuary; books and robes. All with total personal service and love of the Goddess. Send $3.00 for catalogue and oil or incense of your choice.

ROSEWYND'S SIMPLES
453 Proctor Road
Manchester, NH 03109
Oils and incenses for ritual and magickal use. She also has handcrafted wood amulets, runes, bath salts, wands, and other magickal items as they become available. Nearly everything in the catalogue is made by Rosewynd or other Witches personally known to her. Please include a large SASE when requesting a catalogue.

THE SAGE GARDEN/ARTEMESIA'S MAGICK!
P. O. Box 144
Payette, ID 83661
(208) 454-2026

The Sage Garden offers a wide listing of occult oils, perfumes, bath salts, incenses, personal care products, and more! Statues, ritual garb, blades, natural beeswax also offered. All of our products are made from 100 percent pure oils and resins. (We only use cruelty-free synthetic animal scents.) Special orders are welcome. Tarot and past-life readings by phone or mail. Catalogue: $3.00 (partly refunded). *Artemesia's Magick!* is a new Pan Pagan quarterly. One-year subscription: $12.00.

SHADOW ENTERPRISES
P. O. Box 18094
Columbus, OH 43218
We offer the finest goods available made by Pagans for Pagans, including ritual tools, hand-blended incenses and oils, one-of-a-kind items, crystals and minerals, rare collectibles, jewelry; custom work services; new, used, and rare books; and so much more! Please send $1.00 for more information or $3.00 for a catalogue.

SHELL'S MYSTICAL OILS, CHARMS, AND BREWS
P. O. Box 691646
Stockton, CA 95269-1646
(209) 464-9764
We at Shell's pride ourselves on bringing to you the highest quality merchandise. We make our own line of occult oils. We also carry over 300 different herbs, some of which are very hard to find. Made-to-order full-length ritual robes and capes. Also, incenses, tinctures, candles, altar covers, stones, charms, bags, and much more. Catalogue: $2.00.

STAR SAGE
A complete astrological service. We offer in-depth personal life readings, compatibility reports, progressed reports addressing a specific concern or area of life, and more. Using the latest in astrological technology we construct natal

charts and carefully delineate the data to unfold the intricate pattern of a person's life as reflected by the heavens. Call 1-800-STARSAGE for a free brochure and order form, or write to Star Sage, P. O. Box 342, East Machias, ME 04630.

WHITE LIGHT PENTACLES/SACRED SPIRIT PRODUCTS
P. O. Box 8163
Salem, MA 01971-8163
Distributors of thousands of magickal supplies for you to choose from. We feature sacred symbolic jewelry, herbal and gemstone spell candles, ritual incenses and oils, talismans, and gargoyles, along with a beautiful array of wonderful offerings to adorn your Pagan, Wiccan, and/or Thelemic household altar or shrine. Send $3.00 for our mail order catalogue. Magickal businesses will receive our complimentary wholesale catalogue packet by calling 1-800-MASTERY.

THE WIZARD
425 Kings Highway East
Fairfield, CT 06430
(203) 367-6355
New Age-Metaphysical bookstore. Ritual candles and oils, jewelry, crystals, incense, burners, collectibles, herbal service, pewter, tarot, small statuary. Readers and lecturers. Light, airy, relaxed, friendly atmosphere. Call for directions and hours.

Bibliography

Adler, Margot. *Drawing Down the Moon.* Boston, MA: Beacon Press, 1986.

Brasch, R. *Strange Customs: How Did They Begin?* New York, NY: David McKay Company, Inc., 1976.

Budge, E. A. Wallis. *Amulets and Talismans.* New York, NY: University Books, 1961.

Crowley, Aleister. *Magick in Theory and Practice.* New York, NY: Dover Publications, 1976.

Cunningham, Scott. *Wicca—A Guide for the Solitary Practitioner.* St. Paul, MN: Llewellyn Publications, 1988.

Dunwich, Gerina. *Candlelight Spells.* Secaucus, NJ: Citadel Press, 1988.

Dunwich, Gerina. *The Concise Lexicon of the Occult.* Secaucus, NJ: Citadel Press, 1990.

Dunwich, Gerina. *The Magick of Candle Burning.* Secaucus, NJ: Citadel Press, 1989.

Dunwich, Gerina. *The Secrets of Love Magick.* Secaucus, NJ: Citadel Press, 1992.

Dunwich, Gerina. *Wicca Craft.* Secaucus, NJ: Citadel Press, 1991.

Frazer, James G. *The Golden Bough.* New York, NY: Avenel Books, 1981.

Gibson, Walter B. and Litzka R. Gibson. *The Complete Illus-*

trated Book of the Psychic Sciences. New York, NY: Pocket Books, 1966.

Gonzalez-Wippler, Migene. *The Complete Book of Amulets and Talismans.* St. Paul, MN: Llewellyn Publications, 1991.

Guiley, Rosemary Ellen. *Harper's Encyclopedia of Mystical and Paranormal Experience.* New York, NY: Harper-SanFrancisco, a division of HarperCollins Publishers, 1991.

Leach, Maria and Jerome Fried, editors. *Funk and Wagnalls Standard Dictionary of Folklore, Mythology and Legend.* New York, NY: Harper and Row, 1984.

Loewe, Michael and Carmen Blacker. *Oracles and Divination.* Boulder, CO: Shambhala, 1981.

Macrone, Michael. *By Jove!* New York, NY: HarperCollins Publishers, Inc., 1992.

Mair, Lucy. *Witchcraft.* New York, NY: McGraw-Hill, 1969.

Morrison, Sarah Lyddon. *Modern Witch's Dreambook.* Secaucus, NJ: Citadel Press, 1990.

Pelton, Robert Wayne. *The Complete Book of Dream Interpretation.* Englewood Cliffs, NJ: Prentice-Hall, 1987.

Sarnoff, Jane and Reynold Ruffins. *Take Warning! A Book of Superstitions.* New York, NY: Charles Scribner's Sons, 1978.

Schwartz, Alvin. *Telling Fortunes: Love Magic, Dreams, Signs, and Other Ways to Learn the Future.* New York, NY: J.B. Lippincott, 1987.

Starhawk. *The Spiral Dance.* San Fransisco, CA: Harper and Row, 1979.

Valiente, Doreen. *An ABC of Witchcraft Past and Present.* New York, NY: St. Martin's Press, 1973.

Valiente, Doreen. *Natural Magic.* New York, NY: St. Martin's Press, 1975.

Valiente, Doreen. *Witchcraft for Tomorrow.* Custer, WA: Phoenix Publishing, 1978.

Index

About the Author

GERINA DUNWICH was born on December 27, 1959, under the sign of Capricorn with a Taurus rising. She is a self-dedicated Witch, cat-lover, poet, professional astrologer and student of the Occult arts.

She has written many newspaper and magazine articles and is the author of *Candlelight Spells* and *Wicca Craft.* She has appeared on numerous radio talk shows across the United States and Canada, and her Goddess-inspired poetry has been published in many publications including *Circle, The Georgian Newsletter, The Kindred Spirit, Mystic Muse, The Poet, The White Light* and *Xenomorph.*

She is a member of the American Biographical Institute Board of Advisors, and is listed in a number of reference works including *Who's Who in the East, Personalities of America* and *Crossroads: Who's Who of the Magickal Community.*

Gerina lives in southern California, where she edits and publishes *Golden Isis,* a Wiccan literary journal of mystical poetry and Pagan art.